Collage creations

BARBARA MATTHIESSEN, KIM BALLOR AND TRACIA WILLIAMS

NORTH LIGHT BOOKS

CINCINNATI, OHIO

www.artistsnetwork.com

Collage
creations

08 07 06 05 04   5 4 3 2 1

Library of Congress Cataloging-in-Publication Division

Matthiessen, Barbara
   Collage Creations / Barbara Matthiessen, Kim Ballor and Tracia Williams
      p. cm
   ISBN 1-58180-546-2 (pbk. : alk. paper)
   1. Collage. I. Ballor, Kim. II. Williams, Tracia. III. Title.

   TT910.M28 2004
   702'.81'2--dc22

                        2003064965

Editor: David Oeters
Designer: Joanna Detz
Layout Artist: Kathy Gardner
Production Coordinator: Sara Dumford
Photographers: Christine Polomsky and Al Parrish
Photo Stylist: Mary Barnes Clark

METRIC CONVERSION CHART

TO CONVERT	TO	MULTIPLY BY
Inches	Centimeters	2.54
Centimeters	Inches	0.4
Feet	Centimeters	30.5
Centimeters	Feet	0.03
Yards	Meters	0.9
Meters	Yards	1.1
Sq. Inches	Sq. Centimeters	6.45
Sq. Centimeters	Sq. Inches	0.16
Sq. Feet	Sq. Meters	0.09
Sq. Meters	Sq. Feet	10.8
Sq. Yards	Sq. Meters	0.8
Sq. Meters	Sq. Yards	1.2
Pounds	Kilograms	0.45
Kilograms	Pounds	2.2
Ounces	Grams	28.4
Grams	Ounces	0.04

Dedication

TO ART'S ANGELS,

WHO ALLOW US

TO LAUGH

AND CREATE

TO OUR HEARTS' CONTENT.

WWW.8ANGELS4ART.COM

About the Authors

Barbara Matthiessen's design work covers a wide range of styles and mediums. She has written forty-three booklets, contributed to nineteen multi-artist books and has done countless designs for magazines. While continuing to design for publication, she also develops kits, project sheets and sales models for manufacturers. Barbara lives in the Pacific Northwest.

Kim Ballor has worked in the craft and creative industries for almost twenty years as an author, teacher and designer of projects and new products. She works in a variety of mediums, but her favorite is beads, and she is a lampwork beadmaker as well as a jewelry designer. Kim has published articles in numerous craft magazines and has appeared on almost every craft TV show. Kim lives and works in beautiful Plymouth, Michigan.

Tracia Williams is a product developer and marketing/merchandising consultant in the craft and creative industries. She has authored columns for several different national craft magazines, as well as producing and demonstrating "how to" segments for several home and craft TV shows. Tracia has placed over a thousand designs in the media. Just for fun, she does mixed-media art and creates with beads! She lives in sunny Orlando, Florida, with her four children and a very encouraging business partner and husband named Chris.

Acknowledgments

MANY THANKS GO TO OUR FAMILIES, WHO PUT UP WITH OUR ABSENCES WHILE WE LOCKED OURSELVES AWAY FOR THE CREATIVE PROCESS. THANKS ALSO GO TO DAVID OETERS, OUR EDITOR, WHO NOT ONLY CALMLY DEALT WITH ONE ARTISTIC TEMPERAMENT, BUT THREE, AND TO CHRISTINE POLOMSKY WHO DID AMAZING THINGS IN PHOTOGRAPHING OUR WORK.

table of contents

collage creation

A collage is a piece of art composed by combining various materials not normally associated with one another in a visually interesting manner. It was that definition, and the spirit of collaboration, that helped guide us as we worked together on this book.

This book has been written by the three of us: Barbara, Kim and Tracia. It is unusual for three creative people to collaborate on such a project, but for us, three brains are better than one. Working together starts a brainstorming process that delivers more great ideas than we have time to get on paper. We bring varied experiences to this book. Barbara has worked in every craft you can imagine, Kim is the embellisher with a background in beading, and Tracia is a painter extraordinaire. In total, we have forty-six years of experience designing in the craft industry.

This book, we hope, has become a collage of our talents and interests, combined in a visually interesting and informative manner. We love collage and know you will too!

What we would like you to learn from reading this book is that collage is not just a project for kids. Collage is an art form—an art form that all of us can do. Even if you do not consider yourself an artist, you can easily make collage pieces to give as gifts, or for decorating your home.

Begin by using techniques you already know, such as tearing paper, gluing and simple painting. You will be amazed at how these basic techniques come together to make a collage. In this book, we will add some very simple new techniques to your repertoire. By combining these techniques with dramatic colors and your personal ephemera, you will be making fabulous one-of-a-kind collage art in no time!

materials and tools >

You can use just about anything to create a collage, but, to get you started, these are some basic tools and materials we use to create collages.

Paints: Acrylic paints can be selected for quality (which you can generally tell by the price), or by color. Acrylic paint is opaque and can be found in matte, gloss, glitters and metallics.

Glazes: Glazes are transparent and take a little longer to dry, making them good for blending colors.

Rubber Stamps, Inks and Embossing Powders: Rubber stamps come unmounted or mounted on wood or foam, and may be purchased individually or in sets. There are three kinds of stamping inks: dye-based, pigment-based and solvent-based. Dye-based inks dry easily on any surface; pigment-based inks stay wet for a longer period of time. Solvent-based inks stick permanently to nonporous surfaces like glass or ceramics. If you are embossing with powders, use a pigment-based ink. Embossing powders come in several different colors and finishes, and can add color and texture to your stamped images. Sprinkle embossing powder over your pigment ink stamped image, shake off the excess powder and heat the powder with a heat gun.

Glues and Adhesives: For lightweight papers, a glue stick may be used. For medium-weight materials use a white craft glue or spray mount glue. For heavyweight materials, use a solvent-based glue. For fabrics, use a glue made specifically for fabrics. For most adhesive jobs in this book we use a découpage medium. Dimensional Magic is a specific type of adhesive that is both a thick glue and sealer. It dries dimensional and hard. We often use it for techniques like Dump Art and to add a clear

dimension to stamped images. Glue may be applied with a brush, a palette knife or an old credit card. Before gluing, consider the material; some papers will buckle if the glue is too wet. Cover the entire back of the object to be glued. Applying glue to the edges will go a long way toward holding the object down permanently.

Gel Medium: Gel medium is a versatile product. It may be used to adhere paper to paper, canvas, bisque or wood. It has a milky color when first applied, but dries clear. It can also be used as a sealer over your artwork. When acrylic paint is added to gel medium, it creates a transparent glaze that can be applied to surfaces for tinting. Gel medium comes in matte and gloss finishes. Remember that the gloss finish will appear glossy everywhere it is applied, while the matte dries undetectable.

Decorative Papers: Handmade papers add texture and elegance to your work. They can be found at craft stores. Also try using scrapbooking paper and paper ephemera such as pages from old books or ledgers. Papers can be glued or découpaged to your work, and can be an excellent background or embellishment to your projects.

Finishes: To seal and protect your artwork and to make sure the inks, glues and paints you use on your collage don't run or stay sticky, you can use a finish. Spray finishes come in matte, satin, pearl and gloss, and should be used outdoors. Brush-on finishes can be used to target specific areas if you don't want to cover everything. Sealing can be done with a découpage medium or gel medium. There are also some pour-on finishes that will give you a thick resin-like finish.

Computer: From researching online to writing text to printing pictures and graphics, the computer is a great tool for any collage artist.

Tip YOU CAN MAKE YOUR OWN GLAZES BY MIXING ANY ACRYLIC PAINT WITH A CLEAR GLAZING MEDIUM. SEE PAGE 23 FOR MORE INFORMATION ON GLAZES.

Clockwise from top: acrylic paint, Dimensional Magic, white craft glue, découpage medium, everyday items such as a scissors, colored pencils, paintbrush and a craft knife, and paper ephemera, collage papers and handmade papers.

Printer and Copy Machine: You will find that the techniques we teach you for photo transfer will make a copy machine very valuable. When printing copies to use in your collage, be sure to use a machine that copies with toner, which is permanent and will not run when wet.

Everyday Tools: Simple but useful tools may be gathered from home: scissors, a hacksaw blade, paintbrushes, colored pencils, markers and a craft knife.

found objects >

Make your collages unique, meaningful or just more fun with objects you find. Sometimes you may find some things unexpectedly; other times you may hunt to the ends of the earth for the perfect finishing touch for your collage. The three of us enjoy the search for found objects as much as the actual collage process. We love to share, and mail our findings back and forth to each other regularly.

Found objects for your collage can be flat, such as pages from old magazines and catalogs, sewing pattern paper, photos of ancestors, ledgers, receipts, fabric scraps, doilies, letters, playing cards, labels, tickets, theater programs, pressed flowers and postage stamps. You will also enjoy adding dimensional items such as dominos, game pieces, watch parts, old jewelry, charms, fibers, beads, mirrors, bottle caps, small frames and laminate sample tags.

You will undoubtedly find items that fall under copyright laws. These may include anything in a magazine or catalog, or photographs taken by a professional photographer. As long as you're using them for your own personal collage, you're safe. When you make collage pieces to sell or for publication, however, the rules change. You will not be able to use copyrighted items legally without the permission of the party that holds the copyright.

Ephemera

Ephemera is the term used to describe a wide variety of common documents, most of which were intended for short-term use. This includes but is not limited to postcards, trade cards, bookmarks, posters, greeting cards, paper advertisements, ticket stubs, receipts and product labels. We use the term very loosely to include things like photographs, chromolithographs, letters, postmarked envelopes, ledger pages, journal pages, magazines (new or old), certificates (stock, marriage, birth), oriental joss papers, bingo cards, sheet music and playing cards. Although it is not technically correct, we include "found objects" in the ephemera category as well. Dominos, watch parts, buttons, optical lenses, seashells, glass marbles, jewelry parts and other "cool" things often become part of our creations.

Ephemera are not necessarily old or vintage items, although there are groups and societies of ephemera collectors that collect primarily items from specific time periods. Technically, vintage ephemera are items not commonly in circulation that must be sought out from collectors, dealers or those who have kept such items from years past. Paper ephemera are the most frequently collected items.

In the Victorian era, advertisement trade cards, calling cards, greeting cards and postcards were often saved in scrapbooks. This was a popular pastime for both the young and the old, and for this reason Victorian ephemera are still relatively easy to find in the antique's and collectible's markets.

Why is it that things from the past are so intriguing to us? Maybe it is because they offer us a unique window into the past or bring back memories of a moment in time. No matter the reason we collect, or whether we hunt for old or new items, all three of us have found that the search for the items we use in our artwork is half the fun. Often we find ourselves building themes for our work around a paper or object we have found interesting.

Tip * Copy your ephemera on a toner-based color copy machine and save your originals.
* Reduce or enlarge pieces of ephemera when you copy them. For instance, make mini copies for jewelry or smaller surfaces. Enlarge items to create interesting backgrounds.
* Store ephemera flat, in a dark, dry place. Avoid storing them in damp areas like basements.

The Search Begins!

Found objects and ephemera of all kinds can be discovered at flea markets, garage sales, discount stores, dollar stores, or in your basement and junk drawer. You will also find wonderful items at online auction sites or from artist websites. Don't be surprised when you start looking everywhere for items to use in your collages. You will be picking things up off the sidewalk, asking strangers for their drink coasters and picking envelopes out of trashcans. Here is a fun exercise: the next time you take a trip, no matter if it is for a day or a week, be conscious of the papers and found objects that you encounter. Ticket stubs, cardboard drink coasters, receipts, programs, hotel literature and other items make great pieces for a themed collage.

There is no junk drawer or storage box of personal items that is safe from us. Once you start collecting found objects yourself, you will look at garage sales, flea markets, antique stores, trashcans and recycling bins in a completely different way.

TIP IF YOU FIND COLLECTING VINTAGE EPHEMERA TOO MUCH OF AN INVESTMENT, LOOK FOR COMPANIES SUCH AS ARTCHIX STUDIO ON THE INTERNET (WWW.ARTCHIXSTUDIO.COM). THESE TYPES OF COMPANIES COLLECT COPYRIGHT-FREE EPHEMERA, SOMETIMES ALTER THEM GRAPHICALLY, AND THEN ASSEMBLE THEM INTO COLLECTIONS OFTEN CALLED COLLAGE SHEETS OR DÉCOUPAGE PAPERS. MANY OF THE IMAGES USED IN THIS BOOK WERE OBTAINED FROM ARTCHIX STUDIO.

Ephemera can include game pieces, tokens, tickets and almost anything you come across in your search for collage materials.

techniques

N ow you have a box full of tools, materials and found objects at the ready. What next? You need one more tool: collage techniques. A technique is a method of accomplishing a desired aim. These techniques will help you achieve the look you want in your collage and help free your creativity. Want to know how to make your papers look old? How to transfer an image from an old postcard? Ways to make interesting backgrounds? The next section of this book will show you some basic, easy-to-master techniques. Turn the page to jumpstart your creative juices and create terrific art collage pieces.

Tearing Paper

These techniques for tearing paper give you a soft, feathery edge that is perfect when working with hand-made papers or when an organic, artistic look is desired. Torn edges add a bit more interest to your collage. Most papers have a grain; tearing with the grain will be easier than tearing against it.

Tearing Against a Sawblade

Lay a hacksaw blade where you want the tear. Press down firmly. Pull the paper up, slowly, against the teeth of the blade.

Using a sawblade to tear paper gives you a straighter, cleaner edge than simply tearing paper.

Tearing Paper With a Wet Edge

This method will give you an even softer, more organic edge to your paper.

1 Fold paper to the desired dimensions, then dampen the folded edge with water. Allow the water to soak into the paper.

2 Gently pull the sides of the paper apart.

Shaving Cream Paper

Try this technique just once and you'll be addicted! It's definitely the easy way to achieve a marbled effect on paper. Although it looks messy, it really isn't, because the shaving cream coats your hands and keeps them from absorbing the inks. Using bottled ink (the kind you use to re-ink an ink pad) and inexpensive shaving cream, you can create stunning hand-decorated papers for a fraction of the cost of buying them.

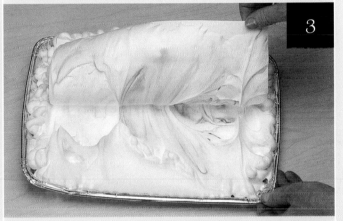

1 Fill an aluminum tray with inexpensive shaving cream (not the gel kind). Add random drops of liquid ink, using a maximum of four colors.

2 With a stick or bamboo skewer, gently blend the inks. Do not overblend.

3 Lay the paper on top of the shaving cream mixture. Do not push the paper to the bottom of the pan. Lift the paper carefully out of the foam.

4 Scrape the foam off the paper using a stiff piece of paper or a spatula, then set the paper aside to dry.

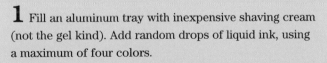

Tip * SCRAPE THE FOAM INTO AN EXTRA EMPTY PAN. LAY PAPER ON THE SCRAPINGS IN THIS PAN TO CREATE SHAVING CREAM PAPER WITH A DIFFERENT PATTERN. ADD INK TO THE SCRAPINGS FOR VARIETY!
* YOU CAN CONTINUE TO ADD INKS TO THE SHAVING CREAM AS YOU MAKE MORE PAPER. MAKE MANY SHEETS OF PAPER AT ONCE TO USE IN FUTURE PROJECTS.

Bubble Paper

Papers with decorative patterns add depth and dimension to your artwork. A soft weblike pattern is transferred to plain paper with this technique. We know of no other way to achieve this delicate pattern on paper.

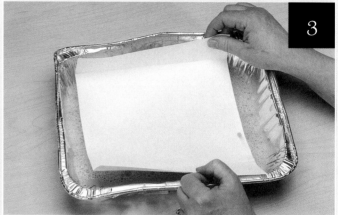

1 In a rectangular aluminum pan, squeeze a puddle of acrylic paint about 2" (5cm) in diameter. Add a puddle of dish soap the same size to the bottom of the pan.

2 Add hot water to the pan, creating a lot of bubbles. If necessary, use a straw to blow more bubbles into the mixture.

3 Lay the paper on top of the bubbles, allowing the paint mixed in the bubbles to print on the paper. Do not drop the paper into the water.

4 Set the paper aside and let it dry.

Tip * USE UP TO THREE COLORS THAT COORDINATE WITH EACH OTHER.
* USE CARDSTOCK, STANDARD-WEIGHT PAPER, TISSUE PAPER, ENVELOPES OR TAGS.
* THIS IS A FUN PROJECT FOR KIDS TO DO!

Nail Polish Paper

Don't throw away that old nail polish. Use it to create one-of-a-kind, artsy decorative papers. This technique is great for those who love experiments. Just like oil and water, nail polish and water are not compatible. The nail polish floats on the top of the water, and the paper lifts the polish off the water, which adheres to the paper in stunning patterns. You can use the same water over and over with multiple color combinations, because the water is never tinted. This technique should be done outdoors, for ventilation purposes.

1 Fill a rectangular aluminum pan (one that you will not use again except for this technique) half full with cool water. Drizzle with nail polish. Use assorted colors and work quickly. Blend by blowing on the nail polish. Do not blend with anything else.

2 Lay paper, preferably cardstock, onto the very top of the mixture. Do not submerge the paper.

3 Remove the paper carefully. The nail polish should have adhered to it. Set the paper aside and let it dry.

Tip MULTIPLE COLORS CAN BE USED ON THE SAME PAPER, BUT REMEMBER TO WORK VERY FAST, BEFORE THE POLISH SETS.

Watercolor Wash on Paper

Float watercolors across watercolor paper to make beautiful papers for backgrounds. Try combinations of your favorite colors. You'll feel like a painter!

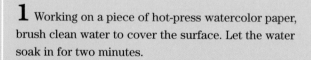

1 Working on a piece of hot-press watercolor paper, brush clean water to cover the surface. Let the water soak in for two minutes.

2 In a cup, mix watercolor paint with water until the mixture reaches an inky consistency. Pour the mixture over the wet paper. You can add two to three colors if you like to the paper by making mixtures with other colors. Spread the colors around the paper to cover it completely. The colors will mix and blend.

3 Add texture to your watercolor wash by sprinkling salt on the wet paint. You can also lay plastic wrap or bubble wrap on the wet paint to make interesting patterns and texture.

4 Wait until the paper is dry before using it in a project.

Tip YOU CAN USE COLD-PRESS WATERCOLOR PAPER IF YOU COAT IT FIRST WITH GESSO, A PAINT PRIMER, TO PREPARE THE SURFACE.

Personal Collage Sheet

Making your own collage sheet is a fun way to personalize your collages and obtain interesting and inexpensive papers. Collect images that mean something to you or relate to your collage. Combine them with a copy machine on a single sheet of paper, use black ink to rubber stamp images and add some hand lettering or computer-generated text.

Almost anything you can make a copy of may be used for a personal collage sheet. Just make sure it is for personal use so you won't break any copyright laws. Try using rubber stamps, clip art, photocopies of people, places and things, and printed material in various fonts.

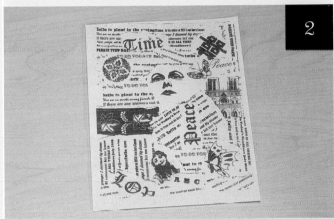

1 Tear around each image so the paper edges are rough. This will help the edges blend together. Arrange the collected images and glue them on a plain piece of paper using a glue stick. Place your strongest images first, scattering them across the page, then fill in the empty spaces with smaller images and lettering.

2 Cover any lines from the torn paper edges you find undesirable with correction fluid. Then make good quality copies, reserving one to make copies from later.

3 With a supply of collage sheet copies you can now paint, ink or stain the background, or leave it plain for use in numerous projects.

Tip * HAVE FRIENDS OR FAMILY MEMBERS GATHER MATERIALS FOR YOU, OR MAKE COLLAGE SHEETS TO EXCHANGE WITH OTHER COLLAGE ARTISTS.
* COLLAGE SHEETS MAKE EXCELLENT BACKGROUNDS FOR GREETING CARDS.

Handmade Pressed Flower Paper

Kim learned this technique from her grandma. It is an Americanized twist on an ancient Japanese papermaking technique. This paper is fast and easy to make with materials you have around the house. Try using flowers from your own garden. Press the flowers overnight between paper towels and under a heavy book. Smaller flowers and those without chunky centers work best.

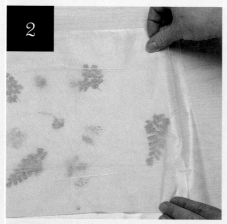

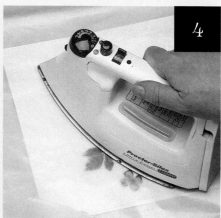

1 Lay pressed flowers and leaves on a piece of waxed paper. Create a pattern or a random design.

2 Peel the plies of a facial tissue apart. Lay a single ply gently over the pressed flowers and leaves.

3 Make a mixture of one part découpage medium and one part water. Using a large brush, gently dab the mixture on the tissue. Cover the entire area where you have pressed flowers and leaves. Let dry completely.

4 Lay the waxed paper on an ironing surface, so the waxed paper side is up. Iron using a low temperature. This gives the paper a more transparent, softer look.

5 Trim or tear the edges of the paper to the desired size.

Tip TRY MAKING YOUR PAPER WITH FIBERS AND CONFETTI INSTEAD OF PRESSED FLOWERS.

Preparing a Surface

Preparing your surface properly will make the rest of the collage process easier. To prepare wood surfaces, sand to remove rough spots. For fabrics, wash and dry without fabric softener. For glass, ceramic or plastic, wash in hot sudsy water, rinse well and dry.

Basecoating

Simply brush an even coat of paint or sealer across the surface, then allow it to dry. Add additional coats of paint or sealer if desired or necessary, allowing each coat to dry before applying the next. Basecoating your project allows the layers of collage to adhere smoothly and evenly. A coat of paint can be the first layer in your design, providing a neutral or colorful background.

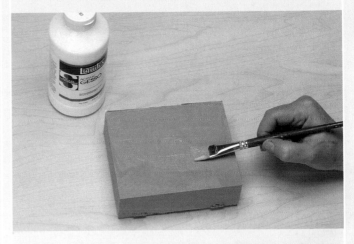

A clean flat brush works best when you are basecoating a project. Make sure the paint is dry before continuing.

Glazing

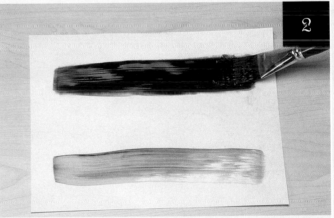

Glazes work much like acrylic paint, but they are transparent rather than opaque. You can purchase premixed glazes in a variety of colors. Brush them on the surface, then leave as is or rub with a clean soft cloth to remove as much as you like. Or you can mix your own glaze. Glazing medium mixed with acrylic paint can give you an almost unlimited range of colors. To make a glaze, mix two parts glazing medium and one part paint. A transparent glaze looks nice when brushed over sheet music or pages torn from a book.

1 Squeeze one part acrylic paint into a cup.

2 Add two parts glazing medium for a translucent look (top). Add four parts glazing medium for a transparent look (bottom).

Stenciling

Stenciling is a great way to create an interesting background or to add accents to a collage. Stencils are available in a wide range of sizes, styles and patterns, and can be used with liquid or creme paint. Use a stencil brush scaled to the size of your stencil design. Use one stencil brush for each paint color.

Stencil Brush

Tape or hold the stencil firmly against the surface. Load the stencil brush with a small amount of paint by dabbing it into the paint and then onto a paper towel to remove the excess. Dab the stencil brush over the stencil using an up-and-down motion, or brush over cutouts using a circular motion. Concentrate the paint along the outer sections of the stencil cutouts, leaving the centers lighter for a shaded effect.

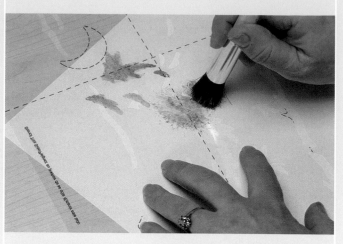

You don't need to use the entire stencil pattern. Paint only the areas you want for your project.

Rubbing

Rubbing is another way to create a background for your work. It is an old method for transferring a design, words or a pattern to paper. Choose the dimensional design of the rubbing to go with your collage theme. Use dominos for a project on games, rub over bronze plaques for a project about your town or a special building, or rub over a mosaic tile pattern or a piece of plastic canvas for interesting texture.

1 Lay a piece of drawing paper over the three-dimensional object you would like to create an image of. You can use any object with texture or a raised design.

2 Tear the paper away from the tip of the crayon. Rub the crayon on its side over the dimensional object under the paper. Fill the page with rubbed designs. Use two or three crayon colors per page.

Crackling

Crackle medium can give dynamic texture to a project and create an antique feel in just a day. You can achieve the look of aged barn wood or the fine crazing of old porcelain, depending on the product you choose and the application. It's vital to the success of your project that you read and follow the manufacturer's instructions carefully. The instructions below are general; check your product labels for specific instructions before starting the process.

Fine Crackle

Follow the manufacturer's instructions for the product. Most crackle mediums require two applications, and each of these must be allowed to completely dry. When dry, brush on a soft wash of brown or black. This will fill the fine cracks. Remove the excess wash with a soft rag, then finish with a spray sealer.

The fine crackle on this frame gives the whole project the feel of antiquity.

1 Brush or sponge crackle medium across a prepared surface. Use more medium with longer brush strokes for larger crackles. Use a sponge to apply the medium for small crackles. Allow the medium to dry according to the manufacturer's instructions. Brush a topcoat of paint across the surface. Paint, brushing once, in one direction. In a few minutes your crackles will start to appear.

2 Allow the topcoat to dry, then coat with a sealer or varnish if desired.

Rubber Stamping

Rubber stamping is one of the easiest ways to add a design or theme to your projects. You can find a rubber stamp to fit any theme. Stamped images add interest and make a great second layer over your background of color or texture. Stamp right on the background, stamp on contrasting papers and glue them in, or add embossing to your stamping. The stamping possibilities are endless!

1 Tap the stamp on the ink pad, making sure ink covers the entire image.

2 Press the stamp firmly on the surface without rocking or wiggling. Make sure the entire image is pressed evenly on the paper.

3 Lift the stamp carefully in one smooth motion to reveal the image.

Tip YOU CAN ALSO INK YOUR STAMP WITH A MARKER. JUST USE THE MARKER TO COLOR THE IMAGE ON THE STAMP, AND THEN APPLY THE STAMP QUICKLY TO YOUR SURFACE.

Gel Medium Transfer

Gel medium transfer is one of the techniques you can use to transfer an image to a surface. It is important that you use a toner-based copy for this technique. An ink-jet image will smear when you apply the medium.

1 Brush the gel medium onto the image side of a toner-based copy. Apply gel medium to the surface you will be transferring as well. Smooth the paper and allow it and the surface to dry.

2 Place the image against the surface and heat the back of the image with a mini-iron. An alternate method, if you do not have a mini-iron, is to let the image sit on the medium-covered surface for twenty-four hours.

3 Using a soft damp rag, gently rub the paper off the surface. As you rub, remoisten the rag. The paper will rub off in fiberlike pieces. Continue until no paper remains on the surface. After all the paper is removed, apply a final coat of gel medium to the transferred image.

Tip TRY TRANSFERRING IMAGES FROM MAGAZINES, JUNK MAIL AND CATALOGS USING THIS TECHNIQUE.

Packing Tape Transfer

The first time someone explained this technique to us, it seemed too easy to really work, but it does! Basically you are creating a transparent image out of ordinary packing tape. Transparent images will add depth to your projects. Layer them over background papers, sheet music and pages of old text. The results are stunning! Tracia's teenagers went crazy over this technique. They now have collaged notebooks of their favorite teen idols.

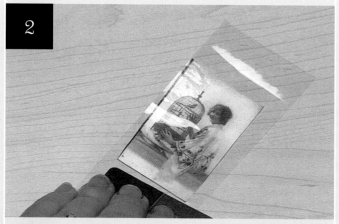

1 Lay a toner-based copy on a flat surface with the image face up. Place clear packing tape over the image.

2 Rub the image and packing tape with a flat object. A credit card or bone folder will work.

3 Submerge the image and tape in a bowl of very warm water for five minutes. Remove the tape and the image from the bowl.

4 With the smooth, non-sticky side against the table and the sticky side up, rub the paper away from the sticky side with your finger. Periodically wet your finger until you rub away all the paper. Let the tape transfer air dry. Do not towel dry because the image will pick up lint. Trim away the excess tape. Use double-faced tape to apply the image to your project.

Tip * THIS TECHNIQUE WORKS WITH IMAGES IN MAGAZINES AS WELL.

* TWO PIECES OF TAPE CAN BE APPLIED SIDE BY SIDE ON AN IMAGE TO CREATE A WIDER TAPE TRANSFER.

Heat Transfer

Imagine being able to place treasured family photos, clip art or other images onto most surfaces almost instantly! You can easily transfer any toner-based photocopy—color or black-and-white—to your projects using a Versa-Tool. Place your grandmother's baby picture on a piece of fabric, or a photo of your cabin on a wood slat. This technique will allow you to add that personal touch to any project with heirloom quality.

1 For this technique you must have toner-based copies, not ink-jet prints. If there is lettering on your image, you will need to make a mirror copy to reverse the lettering. Tear the image from the photocopy, so you are transferring just the materials you need for the project.

2 Follow the manufacturer's safety instructions for the heat transfer tool. Allow the tool to heat up. Place the copy face down on the surface. Slowly run the heated tool over the back of the copy using moderate pressure.

3 Lift a corner of the copy to check on the transfer progress. If the image is not completely transferred, run the tool back over the copy. Should the copy paper start to turn brown, you are moving the tool too slowly. You can combine multiple images using this technique.

Crayon Melting

We love crayons—ever since our early artist years as kids with coloring books. The unique effects you can achieve by melting crayons on a surface are stunning. The next time you see one of those boxes of a hundred different crayon colors, remember this technique and think about the touches of color you can add to your project by melting a few crayons onto it.

1 Touch the tip of a crayon to a heated iron. A mini-iron with no steam holes (found in the quilting section of your craft store) works excellently for this.

2 Use the iron to spread the melted crayon on the surface you are decorating. Add other colors as you like, and use the iron to blend them together.

3 Clean the iron with a paper towel, then use the iron to scrape off the excess crayon from the project to thin the color. Use the clean iron to blend the colors together.

Tip * TRY METALLIC AND GEL CRAYONS WITH THIS TECHNIQUE FOR SOME INTERESTING EFFECTS.
* SHRED CRAYONS WITH A SMALL-HOLED HAND GRATER (LIKE YOU USE TO SHRED CHEESE) ONTO THE SURFACE, THEN BLEND THEM WITH THE HOT IRON.
* IF THE IRON GETS A DIRTY FILM ON THE BOTTOM, RUB THE HOT IRON OVER WAXED PAPER, THEN WIPE IT ON CLEAN PAPER TOWELS.

Dump Art

For lack of a better term, Tracia named this technique "dump art." It made us laugh, so the name stuck! This dimensional style of collage adds interesting texture and depth to a design. Collecting elements to create dump art is half the fun; just go digging through your kitchen junk drawer and your craft supplies. We're sure you will come up with some interesting objects to dump into a design.

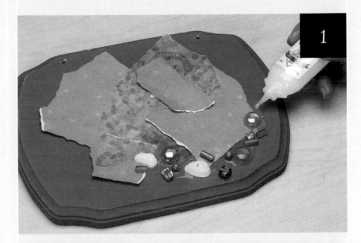

1 Squeeze Dimensional Magic onto your surface. Carefully dump in the largest pieces first, such as seashells, glass marbles, charms, buttons, sea glass and such. These will become the focal points of the collection.

2 Carefully dump medium-size pieces onto the surface, such as beads, gems, smaller shells and buttons.

3 Finally, dump the smallest pieces onto the surface, such as glitter and micro beads. Sprinkle these on and tilt the surface so they fill all the small voids within the design. Let dry and then brush off any excess pieces.

Tip * TOSS ODDS AND ENDS AND LEFTOVERS FROM OTHER PROJECTS IN A BOWL OR BOX TO USE FOR DUMP ART AT A LATER TIME, CREATING A COLLECTION, OR SOUP, OF MISCELLANEOUS GOODIES. USE THIS SOUP WHEN A PROJECT FEELS BARE AND YOU NEED JUST A LITTLE SOMETHING MORE.

* MICRO BEADS OR FINE GLITTER ARE A NECESSITY WHEN CREATING DUMP ART. THESE FILL THE TINY VOIDS BETWEEN OBJECTS AND TIE THE DESIGN TOGETHER.

Metal Leafing

Metal leaf adds exciting texture and provides a glow to your work. Copper, silver, gold and variegated leaf products are available in sheets or flakes. Use metal leaf to highlight a collage element, or add it randomly to your design as a rich accent.

1 Apply leafing adhesive or découpage medium to the surface where the leafing will be applied. Allow leafing adhesive to dry, following the manufacturer's instructions. If using découpage medium, proceed immediately to the next step.

2 Work in an area protected from air movement. Metal leaf is very fine and will fly away on a whisper of wind. Gently place the leaf onto dry adhesive or wet découpage medium.

3 If using leafing adhesive, brush the leaf down with a soft brush or rag. When working with découpage medium, dab more medium over the leaf. This will produce crackles in the leaf while securing the leaf to your project. It will also protect the leaf from dust and handling.

Color Discharge

Color discharge involves using bleach to stamp or paint designs on fabric or paper. The process produces dramatic results quickly and easily. Depending on the dyes used during the manufacturing of the fabric or paper, or the type of ink pads you use to dye the surface, different tones will appear as the bleach works. By using this technique you can turn ordinary, solid-color cardstock into faux batik paper. Or, completely coordinate your project by using the same stamps with bleach, then with ink or paint.

Stamping with Bleach

Pour a small amount of bleach (liquid or gel) onto a pad of paper towels. Dab a foam stamp into the bleach so it is covered with bleach but not dripping. Press the stamp firmly onto the surface. Lift the stamp straight up. After

Use multiple stamps to create a much larger design on the paper or fabric.

discharging color from fabric, make sure to rinse the fabric well in cold water, then in warm water to remove the bleach from the fibers.

Coffee and Tea Staining

Instantly give the appearance of days past to new papers or fabrics using coffee or tea. Age your paper or fabric to look gently worn, or give it the look of just having been unearthed; it's all up to you.

1 Save that last bit of coffee in the morning or brew up a strong cup of tea to impart vintage appeal to papers or fabrics. Place the fabric or paper in the coffee or tea.

2 Remove the paper or fabric, then allow it to dry. For a darker hue, redip the paper or fabric or allow it to sit in the coffee or tea for a longer period of time.

principles for stress-free design >

Now that you have an idea of materials and techniques you can use, you probably want to know how you should start collaging. It's a good idea to gather the things you want to use and lay them out on the surface before you attach anything. Move them around until the design is pleasing and eye-catching.

Creating a pleasing and eye-catching design is easier than you think. You don't have to go to design school to be able to make a great collage. Here are some ideas to keep in mind as you work, or if you want to fix a collage that needs a little something extra.

Focal Point

Create a focal point by including something larger, bolder or more important than anything else in the overall design. A focal point is what draws the eye to the collage. If you aren't sure if you have a focal point, try this: turn your head, then quickly turn back to face your collage and see what the first thing is that you notice. If nothing stands out at first glance, you may need to add a focal point.

Balance

A pleasing collage should have balance, which means the visual weight of your work should be equal on both sides. Balance can be symmetical, with both sides even, or assymetrical, where elements are different but carry the same visual weight. Your work will look unbalanced if you put more of the design on only one side, or only on the top or the bottom.

The watch in the upper corner catches your attention, and ties together the other elements of the collage. This collage project can be found on page 84.

The design elements are almost symmetrical on this table collage. This collage project can be found on page 72.

Repetition

Repeating the same element can make a point, provide visual texture, or just make an interesting pattern. A stripe repeated across the page makes a different statement than one stripe along the side. Repetition can make unrelated elements feel related. A variety of leaf images in various mediums will feel cohesive. Using repetition will also calm a design that is too busy, or give strength to a weak design by virtue of repeating a design element.

Texture

A collage with varied textures will be more interesting than one with a completely smooth surface. The texture may be either visual or tactile. Use a pattern painted across the page, faux effects like combing, sponging and marbleizing, or preprinted papers that look like stones, grass, water or fabric to add visual texture. Adding handmade papers, fabrics, leaves from the backyard, embossed rubber stamp images, thick paint with patterns etched into it or découpaged crinkled tissue paper will provide tactile texture.

These design principles are probably more familiar than you thought they'd be. You use design principles to put together your clothing and accessories, to furnish your home and to plan your garden. Design principles affect nearly everything in our lives because they create harmonious relationships between diverse elements. You can't help but feel familiar with them. When they are used well, we feel comfortable with the resulting arrangement.

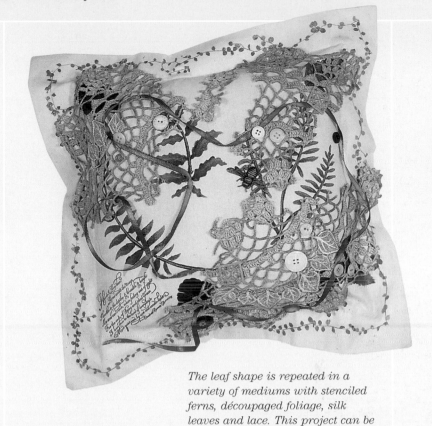

The leaf shape is repeated in a variety of mediums with stenciled ferns, découpaged foliage, silk leaves and lace. This project can be found on page 80.

Layered papers, beads, charms and shells all add interesting texture. This collage project can be found on page 52.

color in collage >

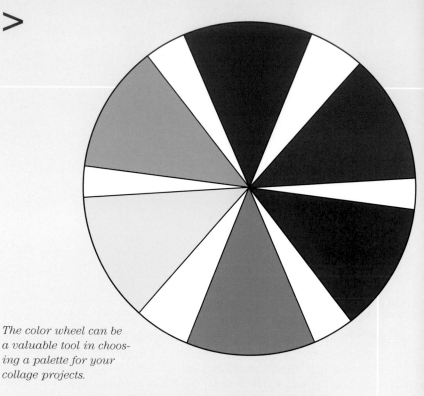

After the focal point, color is the first thing a viewer will notice in a collage. One way to select a color palette for your collage is to take hues from a favorite painting or a shirt that you like and incorporate them into your collage. If the colors worked together there, they will work in your piece too. You can also select colors from a color wheel. You can find a color wheel in any craft store; they are simple tools for picking colors for your project. Clever use of color can really add much to the overall appeal of your project.

The emphasis of your collage might be the theme, but you cannot escape color. Each of the following collages use the word *rock* as its theme, but it is through the use of color that each collage becomes very different.

The color wheel can be a valuable tool in choosing a palette for your collage projects.

Complementary palette

Select a color on the wheel, then look directly across from it to find its complementary color. For example, green and red are complementary colors. All of the paints and papers you have in shades of green and red are complementary.

A palette of complementary colors is the most energetic.

Rock Hudson Collage

Kim's collage has a complementary color scheme with red and shades of green.

Analogous palette

Select a color on the color wheel, then look right next to it on either side to find its analogous colors. If you select blue, its analogous palette might include blue-violet, green and green-blue. A palette of analogous colors will be calmer than a complementary one.

Rock n' Roll Collage
This collage by Tracia has a calming effect with an analogous color scheme of blues and greens.

Monochromatic palette

Monochromatic palettes include only colors in one hue family. For instance, if you select blue, your palette could include green-blue and blue-violet. Using a monotone color palette is a great way to convey a specific emotion. Red is very passionate. Yellow is optimistic. Green is refreshing. Blue is peaceful. Purple is regal. Brown is tranquil. White is innocent.

You can use a specific color as the topic of your design. For instance, if you choose the color blue, you might add to your collage images and likenesses of water or sky. You might also add things that are not normally blue, like a blue apple.

Rock and Stone Collage
Barbara's collage has a monochromatic color scheme.

putting it all together >

Becoming a collage artist is easier than you think. Here are three easy steps for creating your own collage.

* Start with the background of your collage. The background is going to complement and support the main body of your work. Backgrounds can be just color, made with paints, inks or papers. Or the background can be a design that works with the rest of your collage. Words make a great background, as well as something textured like fabrics, handmade papers or fibers. You can also use photocopies, rubber-stamped papers, polymer clay, sheets of copper or tin, or copies of photographs to make a background.

* The main body of your work tells your story, makes your statement or is just interesting to view. Create it with rubber stamps, magazine pictures, photographs, quotes or sayings, memorabilia, or ephemera of all kinds. Glue or découpage these next layers over the background, or use adhesive foam dots to give your work more dimension.

* Then embellish! Adding some decorations to your design is like putting the icing on a cake. To increase interest and give your work more texture and depth, try adding ribbons, buttons, beads, wire or found objects: keys, old playing cards, game pieces, charms—anything that strikes your fancy.

The Artist's Perspective

We want to show you how to take everything we have taught you so far and bring it all together to create a beautiful piece of art. It might seem tricky at first, but if you look behind the scenes you'll be amazed at how simple it really is.

In this next section we wanted to give you a behind-the-scenes look at our own creative process by studying three pieces of art. Each is very different and showcases a variety of techniques and design choices we used to create the effect we wanted.

As you look over these collages, you will see how each of the techniques can be used in the collage. You'll discover how the design principles can help guide the placement and use of techniques and materials of the collage for striking and beautiful effects, and you can see how we use the various elements to illustrate the theme of the collage.

Best of all, you can see how much fun we had just sitting down to create and explore!

Tip A FUN AND EASY WAY TO MAKE A COLLAGE IS TO SELECT A THEME, SPEND TEN MINUTES COLLECTING THINGS THAT FIT YOUR THEME, AND THEN SIT DOWN AND PUT THEM ALL TOGETHER.

Heritage Box

by Barbara

I chose green for this monochromatic collage because I wanted it to feel organic—as if it sprang from the earth. Gardening is another passion of mine and I am often torn between playing in the dirt and splashing paint in my studio. The layered, distressed background and Pre-Raphaelite print give the collage a sense of antiquity.

I chose a medium, fairly vivid green to basecoat the outside of the box to allow the dark and light green stamped images to show. I added texture and visual interest by lightly sanding the background.

I used a graphic square rubber stamp in light and dark green with an overlapping tile pattern for repetition. I found the repetition a nice contrast to the distressing I added by sanding after the paint dried.

The Pre-Raphaelite print is the focal point of the collage, which balances nicely with the leaf and the coin, all of which give the collage a variety of textures.

I découpaged tissue and mulberry papers to the background, then peeled and rubbed parts of the papers off, aging them. They are barely visible, but they add texture to flat, stamped and painted surfaces.

To give my collage a more aged look, I crackled. Dark green shows through the crackles under a lighter green on the sides.

To soften the edges and visually push the text into the background, I melted and smeared green crayons along the text outline. It added color as well as the wax texture.

Creating definition can be tricky when you are using only one color. To help me with that, I did the stenciling in metallic green. I left parts of the stencil design unpainted, and then sanded the stencil after it dried.

Child's Play Altered Book

by Tracia

For this altered book cover collage I'm using the theme Child's Play. I included vintage toys and ephemera I've gathered over the years. Being the mother of four children, I use them as the inspiration for many of the pages in the book. My collages are always full and busy. If the person viewing my collage has to spend extra time looking at it to find all the details, then I consider the piece a success.

The book has a basecoat of complementary colors—metallic olive and rose. Both colors have pearlized gold in them.

Gel medium transfer was used to add the ferris wheel to the cover. It adds depth to the collage as the layers of images build on each other.

The vintage valentine is my focal point. The dump art frame and the dominos help draw attention to it.

The verse complements the theme of the collage and was printed on tissue paper then découpaged in place.

Beads, buttons, rick rack, dominos and other embellishments add another dimension to the collage and frame the images.

Dump art adds visual interest to the design and helps link the repetitious elements like the beads together. Search leftovers and junk drawers for tiny treasures you can use in your dump art.

The words "child's play" written out in beads bring attention to the theme of the collage, and were attached using ribbon tied to the cover.

Silhouettes of the children and the child looking out the window were added using the packing tape transfer technique. I patted paint around the edges of the images to soften lines and create a cohesive design.

Purse Journal Collage

by Kim

I am always thinking ahead to what I will work on next. I am a beader, and I make my own glass beads. This blank book that I cut into the shape of a purse will be a great place for me to keep notes about future projects. This same kind of collage can be made for any hobby. Just add things that relate to your collection or hobby.

The beads on the cover, in the handle and the dump art on the tag all add an element of repetition to the collage and help link the various elements of the design.

The rubber stamping adds layers, color and design to the collage. It also conveys the message of the collage using alphabet stamps.

The words "Bead Dreams" on the left is balanced by the swirl of bugle beads on the right.

This watercolor paper is torn into an organic shape, something not crisp. Beads have clean hard lines and the torn paper provides a contrast to that.

My huge collection of beads and charms made it easy for me to find things to add to my bead dreams collage. I love dimensional collage so I always glue lots of found objects on the top layer, all of which relate to the theme of the collage—creativity and my love of beading.

To basecoat, I crackled turquoise over yellow-green adding both visual and tactile texture. I used analogous colors for a calming effect to enhance the dream like quality of the collage.

collage projects

We enjoyed the time we spent collaborating and creating each of these pieces of art for the book. You can use these projects as blueprints, or simply as inspiration for your own projects. Base your own pieces as closely or as loosely on the ones featured here as you like. You now have the tools to experiment with your collage art and develop your own style, so don't hesitate to let your imagination guide you as an artist. Turn the page and begin your own creative journey!

Vintage Vanity Set

BY TRACIA

The simple techniques used to create this vanity set may be used for other objects, such as canisters, storage boxes or wall art.

ARTchix images were used to create this collection. To create a more personalized version of this project, you can also use toner-based color copies of personal photos or documents.

MATERIALS Surfaces for vanity set: wooden containers, wooden tray and accessories • Four wooden balls (feet for the tray) • Five wooden doll heads per container (to create feet and knobs) • Assorted collage images • Three coordinating sheets shaving cream paper (for information about making shaving cream paper, see page 17) • Found objects: fibers, buttons, keys, etc. • Acrylic paint: ivory, gold • Wood glue • Antique découpage medium • Paintbrush • Scissors

découpage

DÉCOUPAGE IS THE PROCESS OF SEALING PAPER OR FAB-
RIC TO A SURFACE. YOU CAN USE DÉCOUPAGE TO APPLY
ANY PAPER OR FABRIC EPHEMERA TO ANY SURFACE. IT
CAN BE DONE IN A VARIETY OF WAYS, BUT THE RESULTS
ARE THE SAME. THERE ARE WONDERFUL DÉCOUPAGE
MEDIUMS AVAILABLE ON THE MARKET THAT ACT AS GLUE
AND SEALER IN ONE APPLICATION. APPLY A COAT OF
DÉCOUPAGE MEDIUM TO THE SURFACE, LAY YOUR
EPHEMERA OR PAPER INTO THE WET MEDIUM, THEN
SMOOTH IT FLAT WITH YOUR FINGERS. APPLY A SECOND
COAT OF MEDIUM WHEN FINISHED.

1 Using the paintbrush, basecoat the surfaces with
ivory, then let the paint dry (for information on basecoating, see page 23). Paint the wooden ball feet gold. Add
accents of gold paint to the surfaces as desired. Let dry.
Using découpage medium, apply torn pieces of shaving
cream paper randomly to the surfaces.

2 Cut out pieces from the collage sheet and découpage
them to the surface.

3 Glue the feet to the bottom of the containers and tray.
Glue a ball on the lid of each container. Let the glue dry.

more ideas

This decorative frame design uses the fine crackle technique, with lemon juice aging on paper and sheet music. Create transparent images using the packing tape transfer method with personal collage sheet images. For more information about packing tape transfers, see page 28.

lemon juice paper aging

THIS IS A QUICK WAY TO AGE PAPER. TEAR THE EDGES OF YOUR PAPER AND BRUSH THEM WITH LEMON JUICE. HEAT THE MOISTENED EDGES WITH A HEAT GUN UNTIL THE DESIRED EFFECT IS ACHIEVED. THE MORE LEMON JUICE YOU APPLY, THE MORE YOUR PAPER WILL AGE.

4 Tie fibers around the knobs on the lids and to the handle of the mirror. Attach a few random buttons to the lids or tray.

Tip YOU CAN MAKE MANY OF THE COLLAGE PAPERS IN THIS PROJECT. SEE PAGE 17 FOR INFORMATION ON MAKING SHAVING CREAM PAPER. A DECORATIVE PAPER WITH THE LOOK OF MARBLE WILL ALSO WORK, BUT MAKING YOUR OWN PAPER IS MUCH MORE FUN! YOU CAN FIND INFORMATION ON MAKING A PERSONAL COLLAGE SHEET ON PAGE 21.

ART IS MAN'S NATURE: NATURE IS GOD'S ART.

PHILIP JAMES BAILEY

NATURE IS THE ART OF GOD

SIR THOMAS BROWNE

Natural Art Canvases

BY TRACIA

Invite a little bit of nature into your home.

Use pressed flowers and ferns along with paper squares punched from scrap papers, and a favorite quote or verse to create these Natural Art Canvases. This is a good project for using up your paper scraps.

MATERIALS Two 5" × 5" (13cm × 13cm) gallery-style canvases (these canvases have a wide, finished edge with no staples showing) • Assorted papers: pages torn from books, copies of old letters, beige decorative patterned papers • Verses of your choice copied (with toner-based ink) on beige paper • Dried, pressed flowers and ferns • Color transparencies incorporating nature scenes • Two colors of metallic crayons • Gel medium • Antique découpage medium • Double-faced transparent tape • Medium-size square paper punch • Paintbrush • Scissors

punch shapes

USE THE TECHNIQUE OF CREATING A
BACKGROUND WITH PUNCHED-OUT
SQUARES FOR OTHER PROJECTS.
INCORPORATE OTHER PUNCH SHAPES
SUCH AS STARS, HEARTS, CIRCLES
AND OVALS. THESE CREATE INTER-
ESTING PATTERNS AND TEXTURE.

1 Punch squares from decorative papers, book pages
and other paper scraps. Apply the squares randomly to
the canvases using the paintbrush and gel medium. Let
the canvases dry.

2 Apply crayon with an iron to the canvas surface. You
can use one or two metallic colors to get an effect you
like. For information about the crayon melting technique,
see page 30.

3 Use gel medium to add dried flowers to the surface.

Tip WHAT IS A TRANSPARENCY? IT IS AN ACETATE
SHEET WITH AN IMAGE PRINTED ON IT. TRANSPARENCIES
CAN ADD ANOTHER VISUAL ELEMENT AND TEXTURE TO
YOUR COLLAGE. YOU CAN TAKE ANY COLOR OR BLACK-
AND-WHITE IMAGE TO A COMMERCIAL COPIER, WHO CAN
CREATE A TRANSPARENCY FOR YOU. ARTCHIX STUDIO
(WWW.ARTCHIXSTUDIO.COM) IS ANOTHER EXCELLENT
SOURCE FOR TRANSPARENCIES.

quotations

LOOKING FOR QUOTATIONS OR VERS-
ES FOR A PROJECT? USE THE
INTERNET TO SEARCH FOR THE PER-
FECT QUOTE. THERE ARE SITES DED-
ICATED TO POETRY, BIBLE VERSES,
SONG LYRICS AND FAMOUS QUOTES.
USE KEY WORDS ON THE SITE TO
FIND QUOTES AND VERSES REGARD-
ING YOUR TOPIC. YOU WILL BE
AMAZED AT YOUR OPTIONS! BEGIN A
FILE IN YOUR COMPUTER OR START A
JOURNAL TO RECORD QUOTATIONS
YOU COME ACROSS AND WANT TO USE
IN FUTURE PROJECTS.

4 Apply the transparencies with double-faced tape.

5 Add a poem or words. You can use printouts from a laser printer or a toner-based copy on beige paper, or random words cut from a book or magazine. Cut these into separate blocks, one word per block. Apply them to the surface using a brush and gel medium, then let it dry. Apply a final coat of découpage medium over the fronts and sides of both canvases.

Tip YOU CAN USE THE PACKING TAPE TRANSFER TECHNIQUE FOUND ON PAGE 28 TO MAKE YOUR OWN TRANSPARENCIES IF YOU LIKE.

Welcome Plaque

BY TRACIA

Collages can be layers of paper
and found elements glued on top
of each other.

For added dimension try the dump technique featured in this project. I have used the word "Welcome" for my plaque, but you could use a family last name or a phrase such as "Artist at Work" instead. The key to making an eye-pleasing dimensional collage is to place your largest elements first, then add secondary elements and, finally, small elements to fill in the spaces.

MATERIALS Wooden plaque • Assorted decorative papers and printed vellum • White cardstock • Seven round white key tags • Assorted letter, focal and micro beads • Found objects such as shells, flat-backed glass marbles, etc. • Silver craft wire • Rubber stamps: dragonfly, Ransom alphabet • Ink pads: black permanent ink, medium blue • Acrylic paint: periwinkle • Watercolors • Dimensional Magic • Paintbrushes: 1" (25mm) flat, no. 3 round • Craft glue • Scissors • Drill with ⅓₂" (1mm) bit • Wire cutters

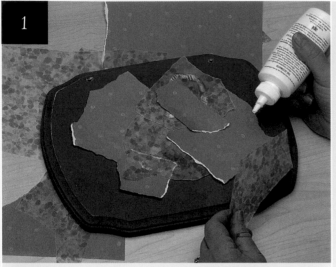

1 Using the 1" (25mm) paintbrush, basecoat the plaque with periwinkle. When dry, attach assorted torn pieces of printed vellums and decorative papers to the front of the plaque, using glue. These can be random and layered.

2 Add dump art to the welcome sign. (For more information about dump art, see page 31.) Use letter beads to string text greetings on wire in the dump art.

3 Stamp six dragonflies on pieces of cardstock.

4 Using a round brush, add soft watercolor painting to the dragonflies. Let the cardstock dry before continuing.

Tip STRUGGLING TO FIND SOME GOOD DECORATIVE PAPERS FOR THIS PROJECT? WHY NOT TRY SCRAPBOOK PAPER OR CARDSTOCK, VELLUM, OR CREATE YOUR OWN PAPER USING ONE OF THE TECHNIQUES IN THIS BOOK SUCH AS BUBBLE PAPER OR NAIL POLISH PAPER?

5 Apply Dimensional Magic to the dragonflies. Use a mix of micro beads and glitter to embellish the dragonflies, then cut out and trim the dragonflies if necessary.

6 Drill holes into the plaque for the hanger. Loop wire through the hole as a hanger, looping it around itself to secure. String silver wire and beads on the hanger. Wrap a dragonfly in the wire as well, and then secure the other end of the wire.

7 Apply ink to the letter stamps and stamp the key tags to read Welcome. (For more information about rubber stamping, see page 26.) Add soft watercolors to the key tags after the ink has dried.

8 String silver wire through the key tags, curling it for texture by wrapping it around a paintbrush handle. Glue the tags and dragonflies to the plaque.

Tip PERSONALIZE YOUR DUMP ART. STAMP THE LETTERS OF YOUR FAMILY NAME ON THE TAGS, AND SPELL OUT THE NAMES OF FAMILY MEMBERS IN LETTER BEADS.

Victorian Shoes Purse

BY KIM

This purse made from a cigar box has a lot going for it. People will not believe that you transformed an ordinary cigar box into a work of art.

You don't have to tell them that it was really inexpensive and fun to make. Add your own trinkets and beads to make it special to you.

MATERIALS Small cigar box • Sheet of pink bubble paper (for more information about making bubble paper, see page 18) • Pink vellum paper • Assorted found objects that will go with your Victorian Shoes theme, such as buttons or small jewelry • Elastic cord • Shank button • Craft wire • Beads to make the handle of the purse • Rubber stamps: Victorian shoes and lace background • Ink pads: black, gray • Acrylic paint: orchid • Colored pencils • Craft glue • Paintbrush • Scissors • Drill with 1/8" (3mm) bit • Wire cutters

1 Basecoat the box, both inside and out, with the orchid acrylic paint. Let it dry. Then tear and glue a piece of bubble paper to fit the front of the box.

2 Use black ink to stamp vintage shoe images on the bubble paper.

3 Color the shoes with colored pencils in any colors you choose.

4 Cut a piece of pink vellum the same size as the bubble paper on the front of the purse. Stamp a lace background on the vellum in gray ink. Glue the vellum over the stamped bubble paper.

TiP CIGAR BOX PURSES ARE SELLING FOR A LOT IN GIFT STORES AND GALLERIES. YOU CAN BUY EMPTY CIGAR BOXES FOR A DOLLAR OR TWO AT YOUR LOCAL CIGAR STORE.

5 Glue trinkets, found objects and embellishments to the front of the box.

6 Drill two holes on the top of the cigar box for the handle. Drill a hole in the center of the top for the elastic cord, and one on the front of the box for the button.

7 Attach a shank button to the front for the fastener. Cut a 4" (10cm) piece of wire and bend it in half. Slide the shank of the button onto the wire, and put the two ends of wire down into the hole. On the inside of the purse, twist the wires together and wrap them in a circle to hold the button to the purse.

8 String beads on a wire for the handle. Slide one end of the wire into a hole. Put one more bead on the wire inside the box. Wrap the rest of the wire around itself under the bead to secure it inside the purse. Repeat on the other side. Cut a piece of elastic cord twice the distance from the button to the hole in the lid. Tie the ends of the elastic in a knot. Push the folded end of the elastic through the hole from the inside of the purse. Loop the elastic over the button to close the purse.

Sisters of the
Heart Purse

BY KIM

This cigar box purse, dedicated to sisters,
will make a great gift for any woman.

It combines the simple technique of rubber stamping with découpage,
and a mica powder shine to make it special. Using found objects from
your life will make it the perfect way to carry your memories.

MATERIALS Medium-size cigar box • Pages from an old book • Collage sheet with images of sisters • Found objects on the theme of sisters • Elastic cord • Shank button • Craft wire • Beads to make the handle of the purse • Rubber stamps: alphabet, girls/women, background, medallion • Ink pads: purple, black • Mica powder: violet • Gold leaf pen • Découpage medium • Craft glue • Paintbrush • Big fluffy brush • Scissors • Wire cutters • Drill with ⅛" (3mm) drill bit

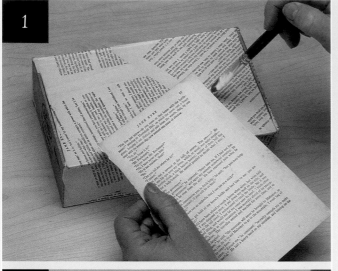

Tip MICA POWDER ADDS AN IRIDESCENT SHEEN TO YOUR WORK. IT COMES IN BEAUTIFUL COLORS. YOU CAN BRUSH IT DIRECTLY ON THE SURFACE, OR MIX IT INTO PAINT OR WATER AND THEN BRUSH IT ON.

1 Découpage pages from an old book to cover the box. Make sure to wrap the pages over the edge of the box.

2 Stamp a background, such as lace or a floral pattern, in purple on the front of the purse. Stamp medallions in purple randomly around the purse.

3 Brush mica powder over the stamped images and on the edges of the box with a fluffy brush. Then stamp the word "sisters" in black ink on the front of the purse at the bottom.

4 Glue collage images of sisters randomly on purse.

5

6

more ideas

If you have one found object that you like, build your theme around it. The empty flower seed packet framed by the beads makes a great focal point. With flower beads and some other small found objects, you can make the perfect cigar box purse for any garden lover.

5 Glue found objects on the purse. Use found objects to spell out words on the theme of sisters. Decorate the edges of the box with a gold leaf pen.

6 Add a handle and a purse fastener, following the directions for the Victorian Shoes purse on page 59.

translating words

TRY TRANSLATING WORDS IN YOUR COLLAGE INTO DIFFERENT LANGUAGES. USE YOUR FAVORITE SEARCH ENGINE TO FIND A TRANSLATOR. ENTER THE WORD YOU WANT TRANSLATED AND THE LANGUAGE YOU WANT TO CHANGE TO, AND, INSTANT RESULTS!

Collage Journal

BY TRACIA

A notebook or journal to record creative ideas is a necessity for any artist or designer. Notebooks also make very nice gifts for friends and family.

This journal was made from a standard-size composition book. Each year, around September, discount stores offer these at back-to-school sales. Stock up! The cover makes a perfect surface to try a new technique, or create a quick collage. This project is a fantastic exercise in layering paper.

MATERIALS Composition book • Watercolor paper • Collage papers (copies of old photos and a ledger page) • Transparencies • Sheet of nail polish paper (for information about making nail polish paper, see page 19) • Cardstock • Aqua color crayons or watercolors • Clear spray varnish • Découpage medium • Gel medium • Paintbrush • Scissors

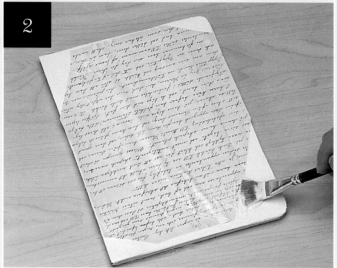

1 Découpage hot-press watercolor paper on the cover of the journal. This will be the base of the collage.

2 Découpage nostalgic paper to the journal cover. This will be the background of the collage. Let the cover dry.

3 Tear, then découpage nail polish paper as another layer of background on the journal. Try to balance the areas where there is nail polish paper on the cover.

Tip YOU CAN BUILD THE THEME OF YOUR COLLAGE AROUND THE IMAGES YOU CHOOSE TO TRANSFER TO THE COVER. COMBINE DIFFERENT IMAGES TO MAKE THE COLLAGE EVEN MORE VISUALLY INTERESTING.

more ideas

Here's a way to make a piece of furniture that is an album of a family vacation. The next time you take a vacation, collect papers, photos and ephemera. Make toner-based copies and create a vacation personal collage sheet. Find two used suitcases, similar in size. Purchase round, flat wooden legs at your local home store. Collage the suitcases using découpage medium and assorted collage sheets and ephemera of your family vacation. Paint or stain the wooden legs, and attach them with screws to the bottom suitcase. Then attach the bottom suitcase to the top suitcase with two long screws, washers and nuts. This is an excellent side table and a conversation piece.

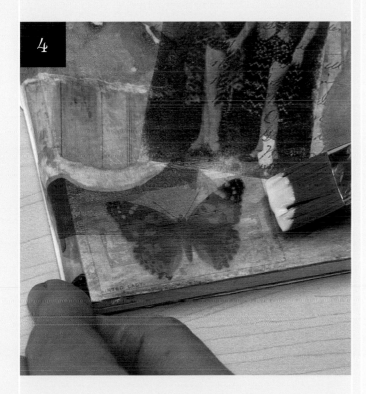

4 Use the gel medium transfer method to collage images on the journal cover. Color around the images with aqua color crayons blended with water or watercolors. Then attach transparencies using the gel medium, or make your own transparencies using the packing tape technique. Mist the book with clear spray varnish to protect it from handling.

Tip FOR MORE INFORMATION ABOUT THE GEL MEDIUM TRANSFER METHOD, SEE PAGE 27, AND FOR MORE INFORMATION ABOUT THE PACKING TAPE TRANSFER METHOD, SEE PAGE 28.

Beaded Cloth

BY KIM

Collage can be done on any surface. Make this gorgeous cloth with layers of paint, rubber stamping and bead-work on fabric.

Change the color palette to match your decor, or change the dimensions to fit your table. Beaded dangles at each corner really dress it up.

MATERIALS 1 yard (91cm) white broadcloth • 1 yard (91cm) periwinkle poly chiffon • Assorted seed beads (at least five tubes) and charms • Large rubber stamps: florals • Ink pad: black fabric ink • Decorator Blocks Glaze: Plate Blue, Nantucket Navy, Deep Purple, Pale Violet • Spritz bottle filled with water • Paintbrush • Four disposable cups • Shears • Needle and thread • Optional: sewing machine and iron

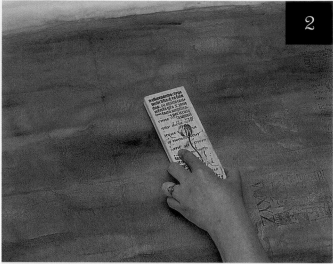

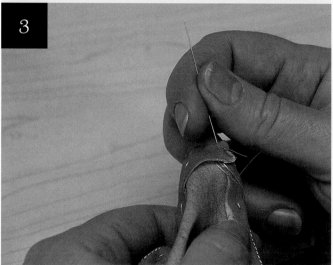

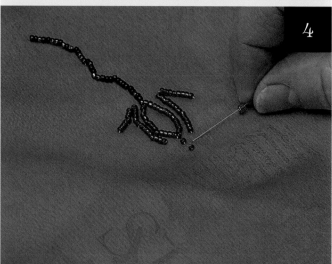

1 Wet the broadcloth and lay it on the table. Mix each glaze color with water in a cup, one part water to one part glaze. Brush the colors on the wet broadcloth, touching colors together to let them blend. To assist the blending process, spritz a bit of water over the painted broadcloth. Allow it to dry, then cut it into a 30" (76cm) square.

2 Randomly stamp images on the broadcloth.

3 Cut the chiffon into a 30" (76cm) square. With the right side of the chiffon facing the back side of the broadcloth, stitch the chiffon to the broadcloth, stitching a 1/4" (6mm) from the edge. Stitch all the way around, leaving just enough unstitched to be able to turn the tablecloth inside out. Stitch by hand or on a sewing machine. Turn the tablecloth inside out, and then whipstitch the opening closed. Iron the edges flat.

4 Use the pattern in diagram 2 on page 71 to add bead embroidery to the top of the chiffon layer with seed beads. Add other bead embroidery patterns in this theme as well. Use the backstitch technique in diagram 1 to secure the beads.

Tip WASH THE BROADCLOTH, THEN PAINT IT STRAIGHT OUT OF THE WASHING MACHINE, WHILE IT IS STILL WET. THIS IS A SIMPLE WAY TO MAKE THE JOB EASIER!

Diagram 1

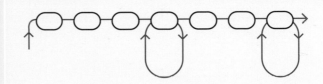

Diagram 2

5 Backstitch a decorative beaded border around the edge of the tablecloth.

6 Stitch beaded dangles to the corners. Add charms to the ends of the dangles.

Diagram 1
To backstitch with seed beads, slide three to five beads on the thread at one time, backstitching down through the fabric at the last bead before adding more beads.

Diagram 2
Transfer this pattern to your fabric, or stitch it freehand. Backstitch the pattern lines with seed beads.

Tip To protect your work area, lay an inexpensive plastic tablecloth on the table before you paint the broadcloth.

Elegant Garden Table

BY BARBARA

This accent table is practical and
beautiful. The same simple techniques
in this project work whether you have
an unfinished table or prefinished one.

Stencil a vine background, add your own script background paper,

then layer beautifully detailed découpage papers over them.

A fine crackle finish is the finishing touch, adding depth and age.

MATERIALS Wood-finish table • Collage sheet: columns, butterflies, etc. • Computer-generated script or script paper
• Leaf-vine stencil • Wood stain • Acrylic paint: olive green, brown • Fine crackle medium • Glazing medium • Antique découpage
medium • Varnish • Paintbrushes: stencil brushes, glazing brushes • Paper towel • Scissors

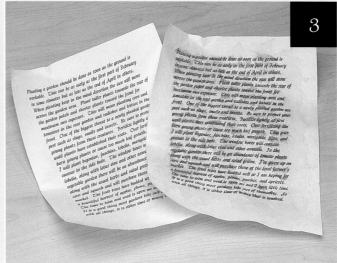

1 Use a wood stain to stain the tabletop a deep, rich wood tone. Allow it to dry before continuing.

2 Stencil a vine pattern on the tabletop and on the sides of the table using olive green paint. (For more information on stenciling, see page 24.)

3 Create your paper for the table. Cut out the images you would like for your table from your collage sheet. Cut plenty of images to allow for creative arrangement. To produce computer script paper, fill a sheet with writings about gardening, using a script font in brown. Print one copy, then make four or five toner-based copies. Dab papers with strong coffee or tea to stain. Set them aside to dry. (For more information on coffee and tea staining, see page 33.)

TIP IF YOU DO NOT HAVE A TONER-BASED COPY MACHINE CLOSE BY, SPRAY YOUR COPIES WITH TWO VERY LIGHT COATS OF A MATTE SPRAY SEALER. LET THE FIRST COAT DRY BEFORE APPLYING THE SECOND, THEN STAIN IT AND APPLY IT TO YOUR SURFACE.

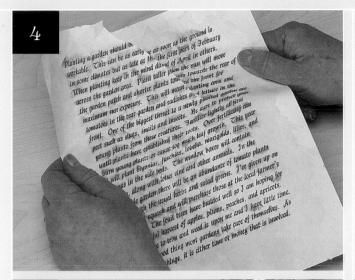

4 Tear the collage images, or trim them as you like. Tear the script paper in pieces a little larger than the images from the découpage paper.

5 Découpage the script paper to the table, then découpage the images trimmed on the table. Apply the découpage medium evenly over everything. Allow the table to dry. Apply fine crackle medium to the top of the table following the manufacturer's instructions.

6 Mix one-part brown paint with one-part glazing medium. Brush the glaze over the crackled top, then wipe immediately with a paper towel. Leave paint only in the cracks. Allow the paint to dry. For more information on the crackle technique, turn to page 25. Apply varnish to the table as desired.

TIP USE THE SAME PAPERS AND TECHNIQUES TO ACCENT OTHER WOODEN PIECES SUCH AS BOXES, FRAMES, PLANTERS AND BOOKENDS FOR A COORDINATED LOOK IN YOUR ROOM. TRY ADDING LABELS, PHOTOCOPIES OF FAMILY PHOTOS OR PIECES TRIMMED FROM WALLPAPER.

Domino Frame & Trivet

BY BARBARA

Dominos aren't just for playing games.
They make great decorative tiles.

Ivory resin dominos are used for these projects, which can enhance
common surfaces inexpensively. Solvent-based inks allow images to
be quickly and permanently stamped onto the dominos.

MATERIALS Unfinished wooden frame • 4" (10cm) unfinished wooden square • Ivory dominos set • Rubber stamps: single motifs of leaf and vine, and one all-over pattern • Ink pads: gold, green, brown and copper solvent-based inks • Acrylic paint: brown, gold • Crackle medium • Spray acrylic sealer • Solvent-based glue • Paintbrush

1 Paint the wooden pieces gold, then allow them to dry. Apply crackle medium and allow it to set according to the manufacturer's instructions. Brush brown paint over the crackle once, in one direction. Allow to dry. Spray sealer over the wooden pieces.

2 Rub the dominos' sides on a gold ink pad. Lightly press the front of each domino onto the gold ink pad. Set the dominos aside to dry for a few minutes.

3 Stamp the dominos using copper for the larger leaf, and green or brown for all the others. Allow the dominos to dry.

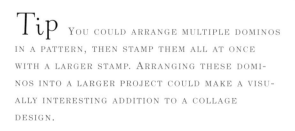

Tip YOU COULD ARRANGE MULTIPLE DOMINOS IN A PATTERN, THEN STAMP THEM ALL AT ONCE WITH A LARGER STAMP. ARRANGING THESE DOMINOS INTO A LARGER PROJECT COULD MAKE A VISUALLY INTERESTING ADDITION TO A COLLAGE DESIGN.

marble tiles

YOU CAN EASILY MAKE DOMINO TILES THAT LOOK LIKE STONE OR MARBLE. RANDOMLY DAB ONE OR TWO COLORS OF SOLVENT-BASED INK ONTO THE DOMINO, THEN ADD TWO OR THREE SMALL PUDDLES OF GOLD OR SILVER LEAFING PEN. MIST THE DOMINO WITH RUBBING ALCOHOL, THEN TILT TO MIX. ALLOW TO DRY.

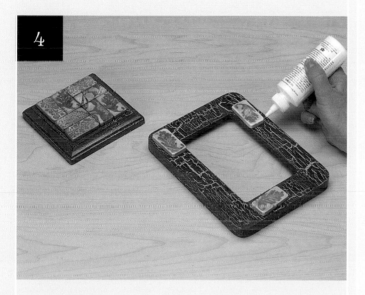

4 Glue the dominos to the wooden pieces in a well-ventilated area using the solvent-based glue. Allow the glue to cure before using the project.

more ideas

Paint a wooden tray blue. Allow the paint to dry, then seal it with an acrylic spray. Stamp the dominos using blue ink and four or five rubber stamp designs. Arrange the dominos, scattering the strongest, most defined images evenly across the tray. Fill in the tray with the remaining dominos. Add domino tiles to any flat wooden surface for a charming, elegant accent.

Tip FOR MORE DETAILED INFORMATION ON CRACKLING TECHNIQUES, SEE PAGE 25. SEE PAGE 26 FOR INFORMATION ON RUBBER STAMPING.

Botanical Pillow

BY BARBARA

This is a pillow design for those who enjoy the mellow tones and complexity of nature.

From the stenciled background and applied authentic pressed foliage to the overlaid trims, this design echoes the many layers found in a forest. Place this pillow on a bed, window seat or sofa, or use it on a sun porch as an accent.

MATERIALS Flanged canvas pillow cover • Pillow form to fit the cover • Tissue paper • Pressed vines • Variety of doilies, laces and trims (cotton or poly blend) • Three silk leaves • Green 5mm ribbon • Buttons, charms, broken jewelry • Rubber stamp: poem • Ink pad: black fabric ink • Fern stencil • Acrylic paint: olive green, medium sage green, yellow ochre • Coffee or tea • Fabric découpage medium • Fabric glue • Three stencil brushes, one for each paint color

1 Begin stenciling the fern design on the center of the pillow cover by using yellow ochre on the leaf tips, medium sage green on the rest of the leaves, and olive green on the stems and bases. Blend the colors into each other where they meet. Allow the paint to dry.

2 Stamp the poem onto tissue paper. Tear the edges of the paper for decorative texture.

3 Brush découpage medium along the flange. Place pieces of pressed vine into the medium, allow it to dry, then topcoat to seal in the foliage. Apply the torn tissue paper poem in the same manner.

Tip MANY OF THESE TECHNIQUES COULD BE USED TO DECORATE SWEATSHIRTS. MIX ACRYLIC PAINT WITH FABRIC MEDIUM FOR CLOTHES THAT YOU WANT TO CLEAN IN A WASHING MACHINE.

pressed flowers

PRESSED FLOWERS AND FOLIAGE CAN ADD A TOUCH OF NATURE TO YOUR COLLAGE. GATHER YOUR OWN FLOWERS AND FOLIAGE, REMEMBERING THAT WEEDS OFTEN HAVE A VERY INTERESTING STRUCTURE. WHITE AND DEEP RED FLOWERS TEND TO NOT DRY AS TRUE IN COLOR AS YELLOW, ORANGE, BLUE AND PURPLE ONES. GATHER TWICE AS MUCH FOLIAGE AS FLOWERS. PLACE BOTH IN A FLOWER PRESS OR BETWEEN THE PAGES OF A PHONE BOOK, THEN PLACE HEAVY BOOKS ON TOP. CHECK THE FLOWERS AFTER TWO WEEKS TO SEE IF ALL OF THE MOISTURE IS GONE.

4 Cut the doilies into pieces, leaving some edges ragged. Each doily will make four or five pieces. Dip the doilies and laces in coffee or tea to stain, then allow them to dry.

5 Glue silk leaves, laces and doilies to the pillow. Balance the pieces by forming a triangle with the leaves; shift and turn the triangle, then apply the doily pieces. Add lace where needed for interest and to further balance the design.

6 Wind the ribbon loosely around the pillow top, tucking it in and around the doilies. Glue on buttons and charms to secure the ribbon in other areas. Allow the glue to dry before using the pillow cover.

TIP MAKE A WEDDING PILLOW USING A PHOTOCOPY OF THE INVITATION, PRESSED FOLIAGE FROM THE WEDDING ARRANGEMENTS, AND TRIMS FROM THE FAVORS. WHAT A WONDERFUL FIRST CHRISTMAS OR ANNIVERSARY PRESENT!

Time Will Tell Box

BY KIM

Turn a discarded cigar box into a work of art.

Choose a color palette, gather ephemera that are reminiscent of time, and put them all together in this beautiful project. You could even add a surprise in one leg of this tabletop box. This makes an excellent display for family heirlooms and the like.

MATERIALS • Large cigar box • Four small wooden boxes • Sheet of watercolor wash paper made with blues, greens and purples • Sheet of rubbing paper made from clock parts • Collage papers with time images • Paper: solid dark blue • Found objects relating to time • Blue fibers • Rubber stamps: watches and clocks, words with a time theme and numbers • Ink pads: black, metallic gold • Decorator Blocks Glaze: Olde World Bronze • Acrylic paint: aqua • Craft glue • Paintbrush

1 Basecoat the box inside and out with bronze glaze.

2 Make a page of rubbings using found objects having to do with time. To give the page more color, apply an acrylic wash over the rubbings. Mix the paint with a little water and brush it over the entire page. For information about rubbing, see page 24.

3 Glue the paper to the top of the box. Tear the watercolor wash paper into large shapes. Découpage them on the rubbing paper. Glue strips of watercolor wash paper on the sides of box.

4 Rubber stamp images, words and numbers randomly on all sides of the box. Stamp words with a time theme.

TiP THIS BOX MAKES AN EXCELLENT GIFT PACKAGE. ADD A RIBBON TO SEAL THE BOX AND A HANDMADE CARD FOR AN UNFORGETTABLE PRESENT!

5 Glue collage paper images to the surface to balance the stamped images.

6 Glue found objects and fibers to the top of the box. Let the glue dry.

7 Glue small boxes, with lids glued closed, to the bottom of the box for legs.

Tip To add a little more visual interest, make a tiny shadowbox for one leg. Remove the lid from one small box and use it as a leg in the front. Glue found objects like watch parts inside the box.

Family Connection Desk Set

BY BARBARA

Make sitting at your desk a more pleasant experience by gazing at the family photographs on this vintage-styled desk set.

Leather trim and brass tacks add to the classic styling, allowing this project to fit into both rugged and sophisticated settings.

MATERIALS Papier mâché desk pad and organizer • 14" × 14" (36cm × 36cm) piece of black leather • 4" × 10" (10cm × 25cm) piece of thin cork • Stock quotes from the newspaper • Six toner-based photocopies of family photographs, about 1" (25mm) square • Hobnail tacks • Acrylic paint: black • Spray paint: gold • Antique varnish • Antique découpage medium • Fabric glue • Cutting mat • Rotary cutter • Ruler • Hammer • Versa-Tool • Paintbrush

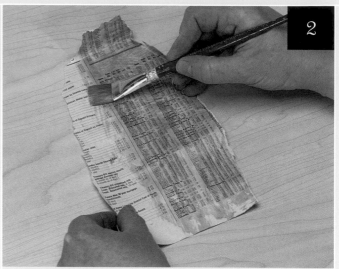

1 Paint the edges of the desk pad black.

2 Collect three or four full newspaper pages of stock quotes. Tear the pages into random shapes, then brush antique varnish over half of the stock quote pages, leaving the other half bare, and allow them to dry.

3 Découpage the stock quotes onto the center panel of the desk pad, balancing the varnished and unvarnished pieces of newspaper.

4 Découpage the photos onto the desk pad. First tear, arrange and découpage the larger photos on the desk pad, then tear, arrange and decoupage the smaller photos. Balance the larger photographs by placing smaller photographs on the opposite side.

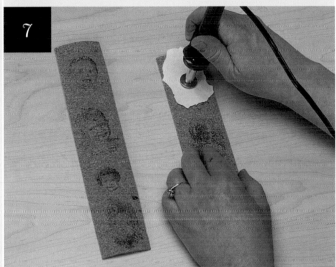

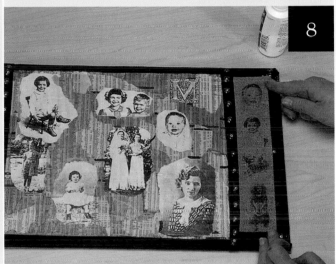

5 Cut the leather into two 14" × 5" (36cm × 13cm) strips and two 14" × 2" (36cm × 5cm) strips. Glue the 2" (5cm) wide strips along the top and bottom of the mat, wrapping them around to the back of the mat. Wrap the 5" (13cm) wide strips around the side panels and glue them down.

6 Hammer tacks in the corners and sides of the leather side panels.

7 Cut out two 10" × 2" (25cm × 5cm) strips of cork. Use the Versa-Tool to transfer three small photos to each cork strip. For information on the heat transfer technique, see page 29.

8 Glue the cork to the leather side panels.

Tip CUT A CORK MAT FOR A PICTURE FRAME, THEN USE THE VERSA-TOOL TO TRANSFER IMAGES TO THE CORK. THIS WILL ADD DEPTH AND INTEREST TO WHATEVER PHOTO YOU PLACE IN THE FRAME.

Poetic Kitchen Office Organizers

BY BARBARA

Organize life's essentials in elegant style with these projects featuring pressed foliage and poetic phrases.

When layered with stamped phrases, leaves and pressed foliage, ordinary file boxes, memo boards and key racks become decorative elements as well as useful items.

MATERIALS Wooden office organizers • White tissue paper • Pressed ferns • Rubber stamps: background, leaf, poem and phrase • Ink pads: green and copper solvent-based inks • Découpage medium • Spray acrylic sealer • Paintbrush

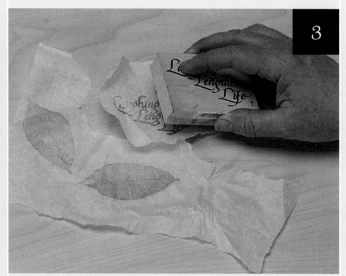

1 Use a background stamp and green ink to stamp a pattern directly on the wood. Stamp in one to three areas, depending on the size and shape of the wooden piece. Stamp copper leaves randomly onto the wood, allowing some to flow off the sides.

2 Mist the wood with a spray sealer, following the manufacturer's instructions for application and drying time.

3 Stamp leaves, poems and phrases onto the tissue paper using copper ink.

TIP A KITCHEN OFFICE ORGANIZER IS JUST ONE POSSIBLE PROJECT USING THESE TECHNIQUES. YOU CAN ALSO MAKE A DESK ORGANIZER, OR AN ORGANIZER FOR THE DRESSER. THIS PROJECT COORDINATES WELL WITH THE ELEGANT GARDEN TABLE PROJECT ON PAGE 72.

personalized text

COLLECT POETRY, SAYINGS AND LETTERS FROM LOVED ONES TO ADD TO YOUR COLLAGE WORK. MAKE PHOTOCOPIES OR USE YOUR COMPUTER TO MAKE COPIES IN AN APPROPRIATE SIZE AND FONT TO FIT YOUR COLLAGE. TO PRINT TEXT ON TISSUE PAPER USING A COPIER OR PRINTER, FIRST CUT A PIECE OF TISSUE PAPER TO FIT A PIECE OF STANDARD COPIER PAPER. NEXT, USE A GLUE STICK TO ATTACH THE TISSUE PAPER TO THE COPIER PAPER ALONG JUST THE TOP AND BOTTOM EDGES. ALLOW THE GLUE TO DRY COMPLETELY AND MAKE SURE THE TISSUE PAPER IS ABSOLUTELY FLAT TO KEEP IT FROM JAMMING IN THE MACHINE.

4 Tear around the edges of the stamped tissue images. Découpage the stamped tissue paper onto the kitchen organizer. Overlap the green stamped background for a decorative effect.

5 Brush découpage medium on the area where you want to place the ferns. Gently place the ferns into the medium, tapping down with a brush that is moist with the medium. Allow the medium to dry, then apply another coat across all surfaces.

Tip PAIR PRESSED FLOWERS AND FOLIAGE WITH POETRY AND QUOTATIONS TO MAKE STUNNING ACCESSORIES FOR A BEDROOM, BATH OR SUNROOM. FOR A THREE-DIMENSIONAL EFFECT ADD LACES, BUTTONS AND DOILIES.

Collage Chic Portfolio

BY BARBARA

Show your good taste and carry your papers in style with a collaged portfolio trimmed in leather.

The rich leather flap accents a collage composed of your personal collage sheet, various decorative papers and a hint of variegated metal leafing.

MATERIALS Portfolio • 12" × 12" (30cm × 30cm) piece of suede • Personal collage sheet (for information about making collage sheets, see page 21) • Clip art in a related theme or color palette (butterflies, botanical) • Bits and pieces of handmade papers, tissue papers • Scrap paper • Variegated gold leaf • Brass charm (bee) • White chalk • Rubber stamps: dragonfly and alphabet • Ink pad: black • Découpage medium • Clear glaze • Spray adhesive • Spray acrylic sealer • Hole punch •Paintbrush • Scissors

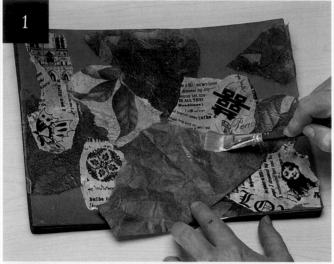

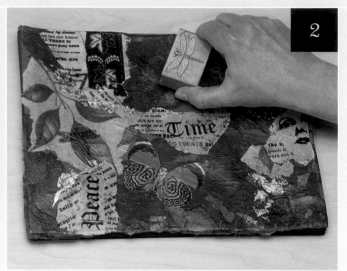

1 Tear or cut images from your personal collage papers and other decorative papers. Découpage background papers to the body, not the cover, of the portfolio for your first layer. On top of that, découpage pieces from the collage sheet and other trimmed images. Allow the portfolio to dry.

2 Stamp images across the découpaged papers. Allow the ink to set.

3 Dab découpage medium around the collage elements. Drop, then press, small bits of gold leaf into the medium. Allow the medium to dry, then brush another coat of découpage medium on top of the gold leaf. (For more information on metal leafing, see page 32.)

4 Spray on two coats of acrylic sealer following the manufacturer's instructions for application and drying time.

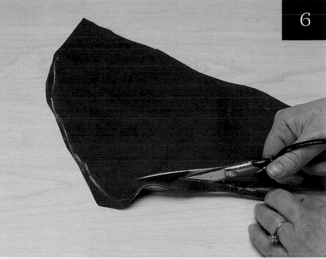

5 Cut the sides of the portfolio flap in a decorative undulating *V* shape.

6 Place the leather on the work surface with the inside up. Lay the flap of the portfolio on one end of the leather. Using the flap as a pattern, trace around the flap with chalk, extending the sides straight down to the end of the leather. Cut the leather on the chalk line. Punch a hole at the bottom of the *V* shape.

7 Protect the collaged part of the portfolio by covering it with scrap paper. Spray adhesive on the front of the flap and the back of the leather, following the manufacturer's instructions for application. Smooth the leather onto the flap.

8 Cut a thin strip of leather and loop it through the hole in the flap. Glue a charm to the flap.

Tip MAKE A VARIETY OF PERSONAL COLLAGE SHEETS USING ITEMS YOU HAVE COLLECTED OR THAT REFLECT YOUR FAVORITE PASTIME. PLACE ITEMS FACE DOWN ON A COPY MACHINE, COVER THEM WITH A SHEET OF PLAIN PAPER, THEN MAKE BLACK-AND-WHITE OR COLOR COPIES. SOME IDEAS FOR PERSONAL COLLAGE SHEETS ARE:

* VARIOUS CANDIES
* SMALL TOYS
* POSTCARDS, TICKETS AND PHOTOGRAPHS
* SEWING SUPPLIES
* VACATION MEMORABILIA

First Step of the Journey Footstool

BY BARBARA

Like an old steamer trunk, this footstool is covered with travel memorabilia as if it had traveled to the four corners of the world.

Rubbing ink directly onto the wood gives it an aged appearance with little effort. Stamps, luggage tags and handmade papers add texture and interest to this useful project.

MATERIALS Unfinished wooden stool • Handmade papers: green and rust • Large and small manila tags • Variety of postage stamps • Rubber stamps: map, compass, travel collage • Ink pads: pigment ink in burgundy, olive green, teal, blue, beige and gold, brown and black • Antique découpage medium • Spray acrylic sealer • Paintbrush

direct inking

DIRECT INKING ON PAPER, FABRIC OR WOOD IS A FAST WAY TO ADD COLOR AND ALLOW THE TEXTURE OF THE MATERIAL TO SHOW THROUGH. IF USING MULTIPLE COLORS, START WITH THE LIGHTEST SHADE FIRST THEN WORK TO THE DARKEST. HEAT SET OR SEAL WITH A CLEAR ACRYLIC SEALER BEFORE ADDING THE NEXT LAYERS TO YOUR COLLAGE.

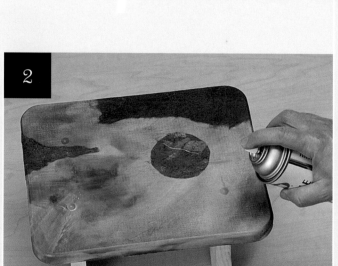

1 Color the wooden stool by rubbing ink pads directly on the wood, beginning with the lightest color and ending with the darkest. Smear the inks together with your fingers to blend. If you get too much ink, remove some with a damp paper towel. Allow the inks to dry before continuing.

2 Découpage circles of handmade paper to the stool. Then spray the stool with acrylic sealer, following the manufacturer's instructions for application and drying time.

3 Tear random-shaped pieces from handmade paper. Découpage the paper to the stool, using the torn pieces to form interesting shapes. The shapes should make the stool resemble a map. Set the stool aside to dry.

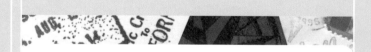

Tip THIS DESIGN TECHNIQUE CAN BE USED FOR MUCH MORE THAN A STOOL. YOU COULD COLLAGE AN ENTIRE TABLETOP WITH TRAVEL MATERIALS AND IMAGES, AND THEN COVER IT WITH GLASS. OR COLLAGE A DESKTOP THAT WILL INSPIRE MORE PROJECTS.

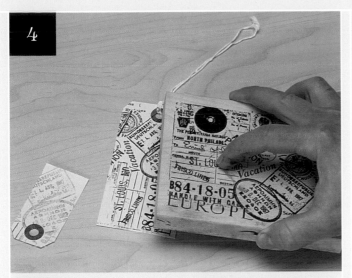

4 Stamp travel images on the tags using brown or black ink. Set them aside to dry, then découpage some of them onto the stool.

5 Stamp maps and compasses with black ink onto the stool, allowing images to overlap the papers.

6 Découpage the rest of the tags and stamps at various angles on the stool. Stamp more compasses in black ink overlapping the other elements. Allow the ink to dry. Apply two or more coats of spray sealer.

Tip MAKE A VACATION STOOL FROM PHOTO-GRAPHS, POSTCARDS, TICKETS, PAMPHLETS, AND OTHER BITS OF MEMORABILIA SUCH AS SEASHELLS, ROCKS OR TRINKETS. YOU COULD GLUE OR ATTACH THREE-DIMENSIONAL EMBELLISHMENTS TO THE STOOL LEGS.

Bamboo Screen

BY BARBARA

Easily create this elegant screen, which can serve a multitude of purposes from filtering sunshine to covering a storage area.

Simply suspend it from cup hooks or clips, or tack it to a wall as a decorative element. Tear and découpage a variety of common and decorative papers for the background, then enhance the effect with linen or wool string and a few stamped images.

MATERIALS Bamboo beach mat • Sheetrock tape • Handmade papers: black, off-white and natural-toned in two shades • Linen or wool string • Rubber stamps: primitive images • Ink pad: black • Matte découpage medium • Fabric glue • Container of water • Plastic sandwich bag • Paintbrush • Scissors • Optional: sewing needle and white thread

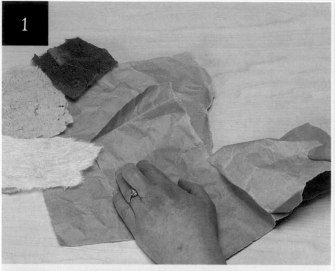

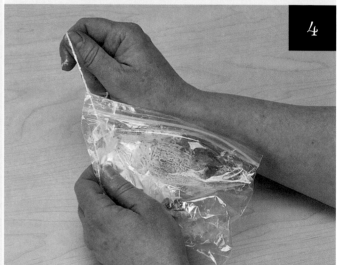

1 Wrinkle and tear ragged-edged rectangles of the handmade paper. Brown paper rectangles should be the largest, natural-toned paper medium size and the off-white and black papers the smallest.

2 Découpage the brown paper and natural-toned paper to the mat. The brown paper should cover two-thirds of the surface.

3 Add the off-white over the first layer, and then the black paper. Allow the mat to dry.

4 Place 12' to 15' (3.7m to 4.6m) of linen string in a sandwich bag with découpage medium. Pull the string out through the bag opening to apply a thin layer of glue to the entire string.

TiP USE BRIGHTLY COLORED TISSUE OR WRAPPING PAPER FOR THIS PROJECT TO MAKE A COLORFUL ADDITION TO A CHILD'S ROOM. TRY SHOESTRINGS OR RICKRACK TRIM FOR AN ACCENT. HOW ABOUT FOOD OR WINE LABELS LAYERED WITH BROWN PAPER FOR A KITCHEN OR DINING ROOM?

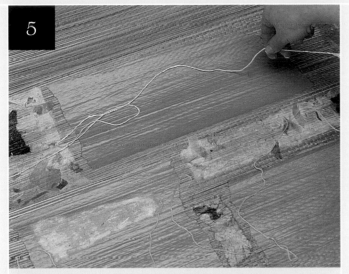

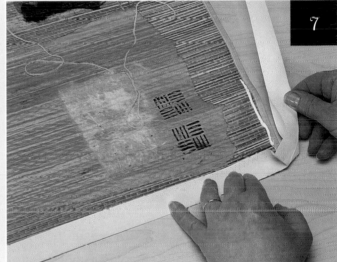

5 Glue the string to the mat, draping it in swirling designs over the entire surface.

6 Stamp images randomly on the découpaged paper.

7 Glue the sheetrock tape to the front side of mat, folding the tape over the edges and mitering it at the corners. Then glue the tape to the back.

TIP TO ADD A BIT MORE GLAMOUR TO YOUR PROJECT, USE A SEWING MACHINE TO CREATE A DECORATIVE STITCH NEAR ONE EDGE OF THE SHEETROCK TAPE BEFORE GLUING IT TO THE MAT.

Old World Box

Storage never looked this good!

This hinged box with the look of "Old Masters" uses simple paint
techniques, a layer of faux stone and decorative papers to define its
classic style. Create a set of these boxes in an afternoon, and enjoy
them for years to come.

BY BARBARA

MATERIALS Papier mâché hinged box • Paper printed with renaissance images • Beige cardstock • White tissue paper •
Rubber stamps: classic women's faces, Greek columns, chart • Ink pad: black • Spray paint: gold • Acrylic paint: two tones of green
• Colored pencils: brown and rust • Antique découpage medium • Antique varnish • Straightedge • Paintbrush • Sea sponge • Scissors
• Craft knife

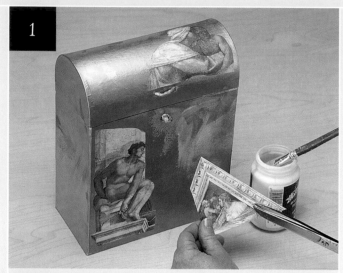

1 Spray the box gold, following the manufacturer's instructions for application and drying time. Cut or tear desired renaissance images from the découpage papers, and découpage them to the box. Some papers can go over the lid hinge and wrap around sides. Place largest papers first, then balance the design with smaller papers.

2 Create faux stone by drawing alternating rows of ½" × 1" (1.2cm × 2.5cm) blocks on a piece of cardstock. Use colored pencils to shade and distress by drawing small lines and cracks in the blocks.

3 Wrinkle the cardstock by wadding it up in your hand. Brush antique varnish over the cardstock. Allow it to dry before continuing.

Tip ARTIFACTS, INC. OFFERS PRINT PAPERS THAT WOULD WORK EXCELLENTLY FOR THIS PROJECT. YOU CAN FIND THEM ONLINE AT WWW.MARYJEANONLINE.COM

stamping on tissue paper

BECAUSE TISSUE PAPER BECOMES TRANSPARENT WHEN DÉCOUPAGED, YOU CAN USE IT FOR STAMPING WHEN YOU WANT YOUR BACKGROUND TO SHOW THROUGH. SIMPLY STAMP A DESIGN ON WHITE TISSUE PAPER, TEAR AROUND IT TO SOFTEN THE EDGES, THEN PLACE IT ON YOUR COLLAGE. THIS TECHNIQUE ALSO LETS YOU TRY OUT A DESIGN BEFORE COMMITTING TO IT. SIMPLY MOISTEN ONE OF YOUR STAMPED TISSUE PAPER DESIGNS AND PRESS IT INTO PLACE ON THE COLLAGE; YOU CAN SEE IF YOU LIKE THE DESIGN BEFORE YOU DÉCOUPAGE IT IN PLACE. IF YOU LIKE IT, WIPE OFF THE TRIAL DESIGN, THEN DÉCOUPAGE ANOTHER COPY IN PLACE.

4 Cut sections of the faux stone and découpage it to the box.

5 Dip a damp sponge into both colors of green paint. Dab paint lightly around the stones and découpaged papers. Dab a little in the open areas on the surface of the box, allowing the gold to show through.

6 Stamp images onto tissue paper and allow the ink to dry. Tear around each image. Découpage the stamped images onto the box, overlapping the papers, faux stones and sponge painting. After the box is completely dry, use a craft knife to slice through the seam to release the lid.

Tip USE THE SAME MATERIALS AND TECHNIQUES TO DECORATE A TABLE, CABINET DOORS, OR TO MAKE A WALL PANEL. SUBSTITUTE FLORAL OR GARDEN DECORATIVE PAPERS FOR A VINTAGE GARDEN LOOK.

Glow of Nature Lampshade

BY BARBARA

The warm glow of a sunset radiates through this lampshade colored with inks.

Even when the lamp is turned off, it glows. Subtle texture is achieved by first applying inks directly from the ink pad to the shade, then using stamps dipped in bleach to discharge some of the ink.

MATERIALS Plain white or off-white lampshade • Nature-inspired tissue paper • Pressed ferns • Foam and rubber stamps: fern, dragonfly • Ink pads: gold and brown pigment ink, terra-cotta and olive chalk inks • Gel bleach • Matte découpage medium • Paintbrush

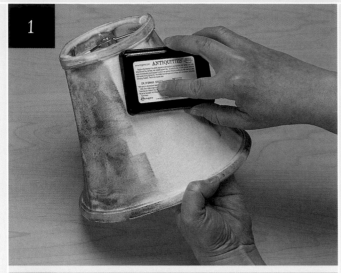

1 Rub chalk inks and gold inks over the shade, blending the colors slightly. Distribute inks so colors will be visible on all sides. Allow the shade to dry.

2 Pour a small amount of gel bleach onto a paper towel or palette. Dab gel onto the foam stamps with a brush, then press the stamps onto the shade. Alternate designs around the shade. The color changes will vary with inks. Allow the shade to dry. (For more information about the color discharge technique, see page 33.)

3 Clean and dry the foam stamps. Apply chalk inks to the foam stamps, then press onto the shade in three or four places.

4 Stamp images of ferns and smaller dragonflies onto the shade using brown pigment ink. Don't overdo the design or clutter the shade with too many images.

5 Stamp words or images on tissue paper. Tear pieces of the stamped tissue paper and découpage them onto the shade.

6 Apply découpage medium to the shade where the ferns will be placed. Gently place the ferns into the medium, tapping down with a brush that is moist with the medium. Allow the medium to dry, then apply another coat over all the surfaces.

Tip PERSONALIZE A LAMPSHADE TO FIT ANY ROOM. DÉCOUPAGE TORN STRIPS OF SHEET MUSIC, THEN ADD A BEADED TRIM. COVER THE SHADE WITH COLOR-COORDINATED WATERCOLOR PAPER AND ADD TRIMMED PHOTOS OR DRAWINGS.

Heritage Tag Artwork

BY TRACIA

This collage looks like it was made with antique papers, but it is actually made with papers I have aged with easy-to-make acrylic paint glazes.

The natural, aged color of sepia is popular in homes decorated with vintage articles and antiques. Using photocopies of actual birth certificates or heritage newspaper articles would make this a heartwarming gift to someone special to you.

MATERIALS Two 8" × 10" (20cm × 25cm) canvases with gallery edges • Decorative background paper: pages from a book, sheet music or a personal collage sheet • Two large manila tags • Sheet of white tissue paper • Adhesive foam dots • Found objects: buttons, beads, charms, watch faces, skeleton key, etc. • 24-gauge copper-colored wire • Four small screw eyes • Rubber stamps: antique images • Ink pad: coffee brown pigment ink • Acrylic paint: burnt sienna, burnt umber and raw sienna • Gel medium • Antique découpage medium • Glazing medium • Craft glue • Paintbrush

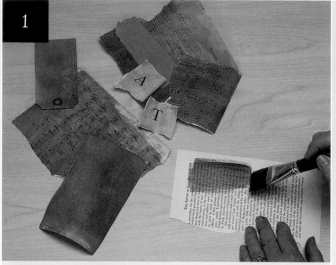

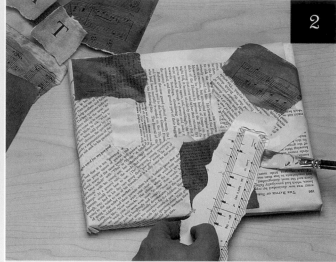

1 Mix acrylic paint and glazing medium to make three glazes: burnt umber, burnt sienna and raw sienna. Apply the glazes to the decorative background papers, as well as to the three manila tags. Tear out letters from a book or a magazine, or use a stamp on paper to create the letters. Use the glaze to age the letters.

2 After they dry, découpage the glazed pages to the canvas. When the découpage medium is dry, brush a coat of antique découpage finish over the canvas. When the background is complete, add the letters to the left side of the canvas.

3 Stamp images with brown ink onto the tissue paper.

4 Tear around the stamped images to give them a textured look. Then attach them to the manila tags with gel medium.

TiP To make a glaze, mix two parts glazing medium and one part paint. Add a little more paint or medium to get the shade you want. For more information on glazing, turn to page 23.

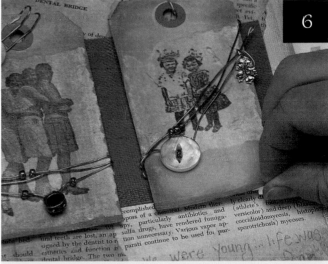

5 Add beads, charms and copper wire to the tags. Keep the wire loose and uneven around the tags.

6 Use adhesive foam dots to attach the tags to the canvas.

7 Use a flat brush and burnt umber glaze to shade around the tag edges and the found objects on the tags. Let them dry. Give the entire surface one coat of the découpage medium to seal and protect it.

8 Attach found objects to the canvas with craft glue.

9 Attach two screw eyes in both pieces of canvas (at the top of the bottom canvas, and the bottom of the top canvas) and then use wire to attach the screw eyes, hooking the canvases together.

Tip MAKE THIS COLLAGE USING IMAGES OF YOUR FAMILY. CHECK ONLINE OR LOCALLY FOR RUBBER STAMP MANUFACTURERS THAT WILL MAKE A STAMP USING A FAMILY PHOTO.

Random Patterns Clock

BY BARBARA

Time stands still only in poetic phrases, so why not keep on schedule in style?

This project is suitable for any room of the house that needs practicality with an artistic flair. Any wooden plaque can be turned into a decorative clock using old dress patterns and gold leaf.

MATERIALS Wooden plaque with routed edge • Clockwork kit • Dress pattern paper • Handmade papers • Copier paper and antiquing varnish (or use a purchased clock face) • Gold leaf • Clock face or stamp • Black ink pad • Matte découpage medium • Easel stand • Drill with 3⁄8" (10mm) bit • Sandpaper • Ruler • Paintbrush

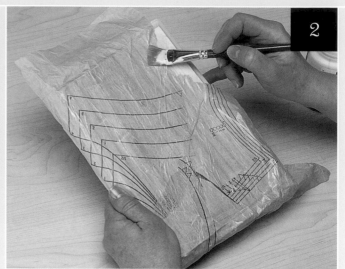

1 Mark where the clock face will be located near the top of plaque. Drill a ⅜" (10mm) hole in the center of the plaque for the clockwork stem. Sand the rough edges of the plaque.

2 Découpage a pattern paper to cover the entire plaque.

3 Randomly découpage handmade papers on the front of the plaque. Place paper in opposite corners and allow it to flow over the sides of the plaque.

4 Brush the découpage medium around the area where the clock face will be placed. Gently place gold leaf into the damp medium, then dab at the leaf with a brush coated with the medium. Continue to dab at the gold leaf with the brush to break the leaf up and give it texture.

TIP FOR MORE INFORMATION ON METAL LEAFING, TURN TO PAGE 32.

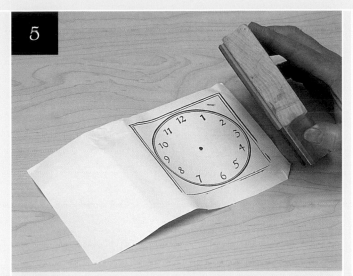

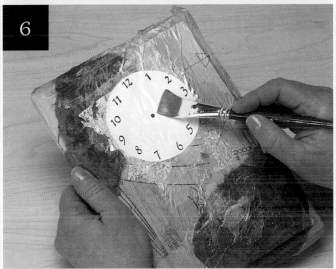

5 Stamp the clock face or use a purchased clock face. To stamp the clock face, use black ink on paper that has been brushed with antique varnish. Make sure the paper is dry before you stamp.

6 Cut out the stamped clock face. Découpage the clock face on the plaque. Make sure the drilled hole is in the center of the clock face.

7 Insert the clockwork following the manufacturer's instructions.

Tip ADAPT THIS DESIGN TO ANY ROOM OR PERSON-AL INTEREST. TRAVELERS WOULD LOVE A CLOCK COVERED WITH MAPS AND POSTCARDS FROM THEIR FAVORITE PLACES. DECORATIVE PAPERS, MAGAZINE CLIPPINGS OR MEMORABILIA CAN BE USED TO REFLECT A ROOM'S DÉCOR, A PASTIME OR A HOBBY.

Resources

Supplies

BagWorks
3301 S. Cravens Rd.
Bldg. C
Fort Worth, TX 76119
www.bagworks.com
Canvas bags, aprons, pillow covers

Beacon Adhesives, Inc.
Beacon Chemical Co.
P.O. Box 10550
Mt Vernon, NY 10550
www.beacon1.com
Adhesives

DC&C Crafts
428 S. Zelta St.
Wichita, KS 67207
316-685-6205
www.dcccrafts.com
Papier mâché containers and surfaces

Krylon
Sherwin-Williams Consumer Group
101 Prospect Ave. NW
Cleveland, OH 44115
www.krylon.com
Paint pens, sealers, metallic spray paint

Loew-Cornell, Inc.
563 Chestnut Ave.
Teaneck, NJ 07666
www.loew-cornell.con
Paintbrushes, palette knives and general painting supplies

Plaid Enterprises, Inc.
3225 Westech Dr.
Norcross, GA 30092
www.plaidonline.com
Paints, paint mediums, stencils, foam stamps,
découpage mediums, Dimensional Magic

Ranger Industries, Inc.
15 Park Rd.
Tinton Falls, NJ 07724
www.rangerink.com
Inks and Perfect Pearls

Rupert, Gibbon & Spider, Inc.
P.O. Box 425
Healdsburg, CA 95448
www.jacquardproducts.com
Paints

Sulyn Industries, Inc.
11927 W. Sample Rd
Coral Springs, FL 33065
www.sulyn.com
Alphabet beads, wire, micro beads

Tara Materials
Fredrix Artist Canvases
P.O. Box 646
Lawrenceville, GA 30046
www.fredrixartistcanvas.com
Artist canvases and materials

Papers

ARTchix Studio (website only)
www.artchixstudio.com
Découpage and collage papers

Artifacts, Inc.
P.O. Box 3399
Palestine, TX 75802
www.maryjeanonline.com
Découpage papers

Debbie's Classic Crafts
428 S. Zelta St.
Wichita, KS 67207-1499
www.dccrafts.com
Papier mâché surfaces

Rubber Stamps

All Night Media Inc.
Plaid Enterprises, Inc.
3225 Westech Dr.
Norcross, GA 30092
www.plaidonline.com

Hero Arts
1343 Powell St.
Emeryville, CA 94608
www.heroarts.com

Inkadinkado
61 Holton St.
Woburn, MA 01801
www.inkadinkado.com

Just for Fun Rubber Stamps
301 E. Lemon Street
Tarpon Springs, FL 34689
www.jffstamps.com

Limited Edition Rubber Stamps
1011 Bransten Rd., Ste. C
San Carlos, CA 94070
www.limitededitionrs.com

Duncan Enterprises/PSX
360 Sutton Pl.
Santa Rosa, CA 95409
www.psxdesign.com

Stamp Credits

Heritage Tag Artwork
Antique photo images
by All Night Media

Welcome Plaque
Dragonfly and Ransom alphabet
by All Night Media

Victorian Shoes Purse
Victorian shoes and lace doily
background by All Night Media

Sisters of the Heart Purse
Alphabet, girls/women, background
and medallion by All Night Media

Beaded Cloth
The moon rose, border and dragonfly
by Stamp Out Cute

Botanical Pillow
Browning poem by All Night Media

Time Will Tell Box
Letters and numbers by All Night Media

Poetic Kitchen Office
Leaf print and Browning poem
by All Night Media

Collage Chic Portfolio
Dragonfly and Ransom alphabet
by All Night Media

**First Step
of the Journey Footstool**
Foreign tags H1848 by Just For Fun
World map and compass rose by
All Night Media

Ethnic Bamboo Screen
K-1778 PSX
Personal Stamp Exchange Home Décor
Zulu border by Uptown Rubber Stamps
Fish by Zumgaligats
Square stripes and broad stripe pattern
by All Night Media

Old World Box
Column collage by Paper Inspirations
Face cube and hourly divisions
by Postmodern Designs

Domino Frame and Trivet
Butterfly time, leaf pattern, tassel, dragonfly,
feather and acorn border by All Night Media

Glow of Nature Lampshade
Delicate lace fern and dragonfly
by All Night Media
Fern and dragonfly foam stamps
by Plaid Enterprises, Inc.

Index

Get Creative with North Light Books

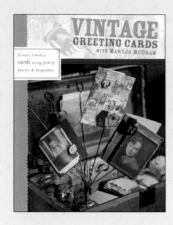

Vintage Greeting Cards with MaryJo McGraw

Let MaryJo McGraw, renowned rubber stamp artist and card maker, show you how to create handmade cards that capture the look and feel of antiques and heirlooms. You'll create twenty-three gorgeous cards using easy-to-find heirloom papers, old family photos and ephemera.

ISBN 1-58180-413-X, paperback,
128 pages, #32583-K

Creative Stamping Techniques with Mixed Media

Make your rubber stamp art more colorful, unique and beautiful! Inside you'll find twenty simple recipes that combine sponging, glazing and masking techniques with colorful stamped patterns. Try them out on the thirteen step-by-step projects, including a fabric wall hanging, wooden tray, flowerpot, paper lantern, journals, boxes and more.

ISBN 1-58180-347-8, paperback,
128 pages, #32315-K

The Essential Guide to Handmade Books

Gabrielle Fox teaches you how to create your own hand-made books-one-of-a-kind art pieces that go beyond the standard definition of what a "book" can be. You'll find eleven projects inside. Each one builds upon the next, just as your skills increase. This beginner-friendly progression ensures that you're well prepared to experiment, play and design your own unique handmade books.

ISBN 1-58180-019-3, paperback,
128 pages, #31652-K

Bright Ideas in Papercrafts

Bring a personal touch to every celebration, holiday and special occasion. *Bright Ideas in Papercrafts* gives guide-lines and advice for creating twenty-three elegant projects using all of your favorite tools, from decorative edging scissors to paper crimpers, archival papers and more. It's easy, fun and fast! Start creating handcrafted keepsakes that will be treasured for years to come.

ISBN 1-58180-352-4, paperback,
128 pages, #32325-K

These and other fine North Light titles are available from your local art & craft retailer, bookstore, online supplier or by calling 1-800-448-0915.